POPULATION
AND FOOD SUPPLY

POPULATION AND FOOD SUPPLY

ESSAYS ON HUMAN NEEDS
AND AGRICULTURAL
PROSPECTS

edited by
SIR JOSEPH HUTCHINSON

CAMBRIDGE
AT THE UNIVERSITY PRESS
1969

Published by the Syndics of the Cambridge University Press
Bentley House, 200 Euston Road, London N.W.1
American Branch: 32 East 57th Street, New York, N.Y.10022

Library of Congress Catalogue Card Number: 69–16281
Standard Book Number: 521 07401 0

Printed in Great Britain
at the University Printing House, Cambridge
(Brooke Crutchley, University Printer)

CONTENTS

v

CONTENTS

FOREWORD

The 'explosive growth' of population in the last two decades has been accompanied by a relatively slow rate of growth of food production in many parts of the world. This situation has led an increasing number of people to recognize that one of the most pressing problems facing the human race today, and for the foreseeable future, is that of maintaining a balance between the population and its food supply. To many well-fed people in the industrialized countries of the world where an assured food supply in the shops and supermarkets is accepted as a fundamental right, this problem may seem to be of little immediate concern. Nevertheless even in those countries there are people living who can remember when their food supplies were not assured, and indeed were denied to large sections of the community. Viewed on a world basis, this is the present situation. Food supply is still inadequate for the poorer members of the population, and uncertain even for the better off.

As the proportion of the population directly engaged in food production in the richer countries falls—and it is already no more than 4 per cent in this country and is steadily falling—the problems inherent in maintaining the food supply become more and more remote to the majority of the population. Since in a democracy this majority largely determines Government policies by its voting power, it is important that there should be widespread appreciation, particularly in the richer countries of the world, of the nature of the problems involved and of the difficulties inherent in their possible solution. For it is conceivable that some of the problems of maintaining a balance between population and food supply now being experienced in poorer parts of the world may be our problems or those of our children if we do not take appropriate action in time.

The relationship between human communities and the biological resources on which they depend, although fundamental to man's very existence, is imperfectly understood and has rarely been considered worthy of academic study. Recently, it has aroused widespread interest, and has been a subject of debate. For these reasons and because of the concern in the University for the poorer countries which face the problems which arise when population growth threatens to outstrip the growth of food supplies, the Faculty Board of Agriculture of the University of Cambridge decided to organize a course of open lectures on population and food supply. The lectures were first given in 1966, and were repeated in 1967. They proved to be of general interest and following requests for the scripts the lecturers agreed to make their contributions available for publication. This volume has been prepared on the basis of the lecture course with certain alterations to adapt the spoken word to formal print. It is intended that the material presented should introduce the reader to the biological needs of human communities, to the biological resources by which they must be met, and to the problems of balancing the one against the other.

CHAPTER I

THE PROBLEM

by J. M. Thoday

In recent years we have been made more generally aware of the problems arising from our expanding populations. These problems are daily growing more acute, but they are nothing new, for some have been aware of them at least as local problems for centuries. Nearly 900 years ago, for instance, Pope Urban II addressed this message to the Crusaders:

> Let none of your possessions detain you, no solicitude for your family affairs, since the lands which you inhabit, shut in on all sides from the sea and surrounded by mountain peaks, are too narrow for your large population; nor do they abound in wealth; they furnish scarcely food enough for their cultivators. *Hence* it is that you devour one another and that frequently you perish from mutual wounds. Let therefore hatred depart from among you; let your quarrels and your wars cease...Enter upon the road to the Holy Sepulchre; wrest the land from the wicked race and subject it to yourselves. That land which, as the Scripture says 'floweth with milk and honey'...

This quotation not only throws different light on the Crusades from that taught us in history at school, but it underlines the relevance of population problems to the complex causation of international conflict. At the time it was written the world's population was about 400 million having grown from 250 million since the time of Christ.

In 1801, Malthus generalized the problem warning us that, since populations increase geometrically whereas agricultural production does not, population would grow to the limit of available resources and keep the world in poverty. He estimated that, given no checks from war, pestilence, famine, or self restraint, a human population might double itself every twenty years. His message was rejected, partly because improvement of agriculture and the opening of the new world allowed economists to forget that soil is capital. In Malthus' time, only 165 years ago, the world contained 1 000 million people.

In 1948, William Vogt wrote 'it is obvious that fifty years

hence the world cannot support 3 000 million people at any but coolie standards—for most of them. Unless we take steps...we may as well give up all hope of continuing civilized life. Like Gadarene swine, we shall rush down a war-torn slope to a barbarian existence in the blackened rubble'. At that time there were 2 250 million people.

By 1964 there were 3 283 million and there are expected to be 7 000 million at the end of this century.

This increase we have to face, but it is all too clear that it cannot go on forever. If it is not to be stopped through famine, pestilence and war, it must be slowed through conscious policy. At the same time every effort must be made to meet the inevitable increase with increases in production, especially of agricultural production. This is the subject of this book; the one side concerned with fertility and mortality and human needs: the other side primarily with agriculture, but also with all those basic sciences on which agriculture depends, together with all the social sciences, for social systems must change with population change, and any measures we propose, whether demographic or agricultural, must be planned in the light of the social situation if they are to be accepted and hence effective.

This then is our problem. Let us now look at it in a little more detail.

Let us first look at the distribution of our problem at the present time. This has two aspects: the density of people in terms of space and the density in terms of food. The distribution of useful land in the world (Fig. 10) and the way in which the world's population is crowded into the fertile land (Fig. 11) are discussed in Chapter 8.

Fig. 1 shows a different kind of world map, in which the area of a country is proportional to the size of the population. On this is imposed a series of hatchings indicating the level of food supply per head available to those populations. It brings out two points. First, most people are in the developing countries and their food supply is poor. Secondly the crowded countries include countries of Europe. Notice the size of Britain on this map compared to its size on the others. We must therefore remember that there are two basic problems; food supply per head, at present the problem of developing countries; and space per head, as much our problem as anyone's.

2

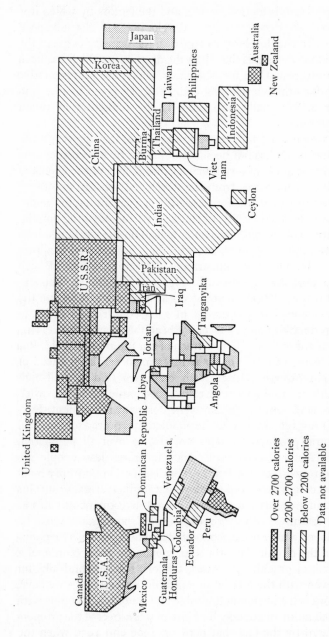

Fig. 1 Population and food supply. Each country is represented by an area representing its population. Compare the sizes of the United Kingdom and of Indonesia, with their sizes on a conventional map. (*Eugenics Review*, **55**. No. 2, 1963, p. 80, adapted from the colour version in a *Sunday Times* Supplement.)

3

1-2

The problem is a growing one, and the factors by which it is dominated are different in the developing and the advanced countries. In the developing countries, the primary cause of the population explosion is the fall in the death rate, which has been almost universal. Data for Mauritius, which are representative of those for other developing countries, are given in Fig. 6 in Chapter 2. Especially noticeable is the reduction of infant mortality rates.

Now we can see from these figures (Fig. 6) that the very rapid fall in death-rate has not been accompanied by a corresponding fall in birth-rate. It is very much a consequence of the export of public health measures from the developed western countries. The consequence of this is necessarily an acceleration in the rise in populations and initially, of course, a period of young populations with a corresponding economic load on the working adults who have to provide the young with food, educational facilities, housing, etc. Diagrams illustrating the age structure of such young populations are given in Fig. 7 in Chapter 2. This expansion of population is going on at a time when we see the necessity of capital investment in such countries in order to bring productivity up to a level per head that may give a reasonable standard of living: hence much of our international aid. But such progress can only occur if investment can keep ahead of population growth. Hence such countries find it well-nigh impossible to attain what is called 'economic take-off', when there are sufficient productivity surpluses for investment. Further we must remember that the population required for maximal agricultural productivity does not rise as over-all population does. In fact as agricultural efficiency rises less people are required to work on the land. An agricultural community must therefore create industrial employment for its increasing surplus population and this too requires capital investment in cities as well as factories, otherwise the surplus population must be unemployed and hence discontented and belligerent. The population of the city of Calcutta is increasing by 300000 annually! Just think of organizing houses, schools, teachers and jobs for them, even with the level of organization and facilities we have. New York is having enough trouble and is not really coping with its annual influx of 200000. The size of this aspect of the problem is indicated by the fact that between 1900 and 1950 when the

4

populations of the world went up by 50 per cent the increase in towns of over 5000 inhabitants was 230 per cent.

The western countries are in a different situation, though many of the resulting problems are of the same kind. Their main expansion occurred largely as a result of improved economic conditions. It was not imposed by the spread of knowledge from outside; and it occurred at a time when much of the world was being opened up for emigration. From 1650 to 1950 there was an eightfold increase in the world's populations of Europeans and their descendants overseas, while the rest of the world increased only threefold.

This European expansion went on the whole with prosperity, for it went with great expansion of agricultural land and of agricultural technique. Even so the cost was high, as began to be clear with the development of the American dust bowl. To quote a 1939 report to the United States Congress:

> In the short life of this country we have essentially destroyed 282 million acres of land, crop and range land. Erosion is distinctively active on 775 million acres.
> We have some land left that has not been used: but it is scattered. We have no large aggregates of land to which we may turn. We are losing every day as a result of erosion the equivalent of two hundred forty-acre farms. We have lost that much since yesterday. It is gone, gone forever.
> The evil effects of erosion do not stop with the removal of top soil. . . In the south-western part of the United States thirteen costly major reservoirs have been filled to the top of the dam with the products of erosion over an average period of thirty years.

One reservoir lost half its capacity in seven years which is the time it took to build. At the same time water tables fell: round Baltimore 146 feet in thirty years. In one place in California they had to sink wells deeper and deeper until they found they were pumping in the sea.

Thus European civilization spread desert in America just as all civilizations have made deserts all over the world. Fortunately we have recognized this problem. We know we must not do this again. But we have been tardier in recognizing that soil conservation and agricultural improvement cannot alone provide a stable world. Population policies are essential too. Reluctance to recognize this has had not only emotional and religious causes. It has also found support in the data for European populations from demographers. In the inter-war period, European countries came to an end of the main period of expansion that resulted from the great decrease of mortality brought by initial economic improvement. In this period, in fact, the population problem meant something quite different from now. Taking the figures from England and Wales, over the period from 1881 to 1931, death-rate continued a slow fall, but the birth-rate fell more

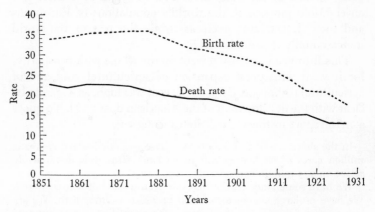

Fig. 2　Birth and death rates in England and Wales, 1851–1931.

rapidly (Fig. 2). Birth-rate never fell below death-rate, but extrapolation of the trends led to expectation that it would, and hence to the prediction of declining population, and to fears of an ageing population and of military decline. European countries instituted policies to promote fertility, of which the family allowance for the second and further children in this country was one result.

As a result of these worries Malthus was a dirty word, and those who persisted in drawing attention to the world's rising population were met with the argument that industrialization was the answer to that. We can now see that this was a passing phase, partly consequent on the great depression of the thirties, partly because of the choice industrial production gave of babies or baby Austins which passed away when most people could have both. Larger and earlier families have brought European populations back into the race and the industrial United States is growing at a pace that makes it clear we cannot hope that industrialization itself will bring the world to a stable state.

6

The various factors I have mentioned affect the differential rates of population growth in different countries. Americans seem to like to have more children than we do. One-quarter of their families have four or more children, whereas only one-seventh of ours do. Similarly, in 1960 both Latin American and North American populations were about 200 million. If their

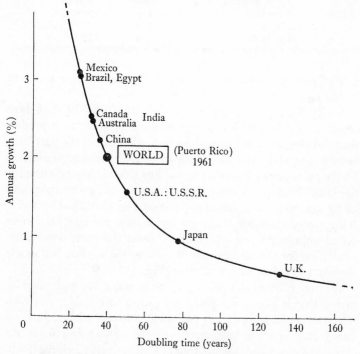

Fig. 3 The population doubling times of various countries.

growths continue at the present rate, however, by 1980 the North American population will grow to 272 million but the Latin American will be 374 million. Birth-rates in Africa, Asia and Latin America run about 40–50 per 1 000 per annum. In Europe, North America, Russia and Oceania from 20–25. Death rates are about 20 per 1 000 per annum in the high birth countries but more like 10 in Europe and North America.

Fig. 3 shows some examples of the resulting growth rates in terms of the number of years required for such rates to double the present populations.

TABLE I. *World Population Projections* (*millions*)

	A.D. 1960	A.D. 2000
Oceania	37	50
Europe (inc. USSR)	620	900
North America	200	300
Latin America	200	550
Near East	110	300
Africa	200	400
Far East	1 600	3 500

The present projections of world populations are given in Table 1.

Such predictions are uncertain, but we should be foolish to comfort ourselves with the large element of error such predictions involve, because, though most predictions in the past have been wrong they have one thing in common. Every prediction I have come across has been on the low side. The prediction for the United Kingdom made in 1953 was 45 million by 1963, and 46 by A.D. 2003. The actual population was 47 million by 1963! A 1951 prediction for India was 435 million for 1963: the 1963 actual population was 490 million. Even the most pessimistic prediction for the world made in 1960 by the United Nations is already a hopeless underestimate (Fig. 4).

We may react to this picture in many ways. We may react by saying that it is not *our* problem, except to consider our own relatively small growth and pat ourselves on the back. But our own growth is not to be ignored—where *are* we going to put our cars and houses and get our water? Can we really believe it will be nice for our children to live in a Britain with many more people than now? Are we, for example, building the two to three large schools that must be provided every day to accommodate our own growth of one million every three years? Neither is the growth elsewhere to be ignored even from our own point of view. First we are an importing country, importing food and raw materials from a hungry world and running more and more often into balance of payment problems. We live on exports, which developing countries cannot pay for unless they can take-off economically. But it is not alone for reasons such as this that self-interest forces us to recognize the problem as ours. Much of the world is hungry and liable to grow hungrier every day. If you are hungry you have freedom only to steal or die. If others, in large numbers, are hungry, sooner or later you will have freedom only to fight or die. It is our problem and our children's problem, the acutest and the most important mankind has yet had or may ever have to face.

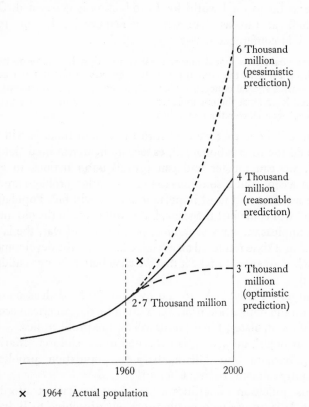

×   1964   Actual population

Fig. 4   The United Nations 1960 projections and the 1964 world population.

And there are hopeful signs. We must not react to so much evidence of fecundity with a feeling of impotence. The first and most hopeful sign is that, thanks initially to those who have pressed this problem before our reluctant attention for years, more and more people are aware of it and willing to concede its importance and concede that it cannot be solved without an attack on both its aspects, food supply and fertility: so much progress has been made in this direction that by now most governments, Russia and France being notable exceptions, are beginning to promote population policies. One of the notable signs of this change of attitude has been the discussion of the subject of birth control in public.

While our attitudes have been improving, things have got no worse as far as total world food production is concerned. One can look at this as depressing or favourable. In the 1964 FAO/UN conference it was expressed thus:

For five years now world agricultural production has done no more than keep up with the annual population growth of about 2 per cent. What causes special concern is that in the developing countries where the need is greatest the expansion of food and agricultural production has been even slower than this disappointing world average.

There is hope that we may turn the tide in time. It will require all the international aid, especially in transmitted 'know-how', we can muster and can prevail upon nations to give and to accept. But if solutions to the population problem are not made our first and most important aim we will fail. Population control will come just the same, but it will come in the old much more unpleasant ways of famine, pestilence and war, the latter for the first time rendered an effective factor by the development of nuclear weapons. I take it that we wish better for our children than this.

And now I would like to end by quoting the dedication of a book on the population problem written by the American ecologist Marston Bates, for it points where the problem lies.

'This book', he wrote, 'is dedicated to my children, Marion, Sally, Barbara and Glenn, because population problems, pleasantly enough, begin at home!'

This quotation underlines a key point we cannot afford to forget. It is no use us expecting that our preaching to Indians, Chinese, and Latin Americans will be welcomed unless we practice what we preach. The Western countries must back up their Economic Aid and Technical Aid with precept. Only if we give first priority to establishing effective population policies at *home* can we expect what we say to have effect abroad.

CHAPTER 2

HUMAN FERTILITY AND POPULATION GROWTH

by A. S. Parkes

My subject is 'Human Fertility and Population Growth', and I want to consider it in the broadest possible way: what factors are concerned in population growth, what do we mean by 'human fertility', what part does it play in population growth, what limits it, and in what way does it change. Should it be controlled, and if so at what level? Finally, of course, come the critical questions, will it be controlled voluntarily, if so will this lead automatically to population control, and if not, what then? This is a formidable list of questions and I should say immediately that I propose to add very little to the millions of words which have been written in the last ten years about the pill, the IUCD and other technical aspects of fertility control.

THE REPRODUCTIVE POTENTIAL OF MAN

The high reproductive rate necessary for any species to cope with the struggle for existence is necessarily based on a high reproductive potential of the individual. A female mouse can produce perhaps fifty young during the six to eight months of her prime. After that, she's a write-off, but she may have left 500 descendants. Even mountains of flesh like the hippopotamus and the elephant have a remarkable reproductive potential. In man, an average family size of four reared children, which would certainly not be beyond the biological capacity of most couples, would mean that the population doubled every generation interval, say every twenty-five years, and I do not need to emphasize the results of a geometric progression of this kind.

Nevertheless, this reproductive potential is, of course, puny compared with that of many lower forms of life; in other ways also it is not as extreme as it might be. In all mammals, because of the elaborate development of maternal care by gestation and lactation, the female is the limiting factor in reproductivity. By contrast, the contribution of the male, however essential, is trivial and his reproductive potential therefore far greater. The approximate equality in which the two sexes appear is therefore highly unergonomic. This anomaly, of course, arises from the chromosome mechanism of sex determination which in turn is a hangover from the lower Vertebrates, in many of which parental care is minimal so that the sexes are required in approximately equal numbers. It is indeed salutary to consider how differently social systems would have evolved had they been based on a sex-ratio appropriate to the relative reproductive potential of the two sexes rather than on one arising from an obsolete chromosome mechanism.

LIMITING FACTORS

The reproductive potential of mammalian species, then, is comparatively modest, but nevertheless it is more than enough to flood the world with any one of them which could multiply without hindrance to its full capacity. In practice, of course, all animal populations are kept in check by limiting factors the relative importance of which varies from time to time, from species to species and place to place. It is easy to think of specific instances. I have mentioned the hippopotamus and elephant. Neither have significant predators apart from man, but the hippo, being tied by reason of its aquatic habit to comparatively small areas of grazing, is limited by food supplies and occasional epidemics; the elephant, though more mobile, is apparently limited by a combination of nutritional deficiencies and organic disease. By contrast, the African ungulates, especially the antelopes, are kept severely in check by the larger carnivores which may kill a high proportion of the young as well as many adults. In the case of man, the limiting factors of shortage of food, disease and enemies have been highly effective over the vastly greater part of his history.

POPULATION GROWTH

As to man's demographic history, let us take a figure used in a 1958 UN report and say that it required perhaps 200000 years for the human race to number a thousand million by the year

1830. It took perhaps another 100 years to add the second 1000 million, thirty years to add the third 1000 million and the fourth 1000 million is coming along at the rate of 70 million a year, a mere fourteen years' job. Figures such as this surely justify the use of the word 'explosion' in connection with the present population expansion (see Fig. 5).

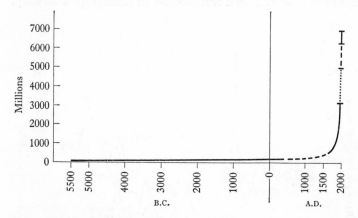

Fig. 5 World population, 5500 B.C.–A.D. 2000. 5500 B.C.–A.D. 400: Sir Julian Huxley, Der Monat, 1950. A.D. 1650–A.D. 1900: Sir Alexander Carr-Saunders, [World Population, 1937. A.D. 1900–A.D. 2000: United Nations Demographic Commission.

CAUSE OF THE EXPLOSION

The reason for this historically sudden increase in the number of human beings is well known. It has been caused primarily by the control of infective disease, especially in areas where the birthrate remains traditionally high, which has brought about a sudden widening in the margin between births and deaths, and made possible by a substantial though inadequate increase in food production. The effect is beautifully demonstrated in that demographic microcosm, the island of Mauritius (see Fig. 6). This process continues in all the developing countries; according to recent reports another disabling tropical disease, bilharzia, is likely to be controlled in the near future. In commenting on this development *The Times* asked: 'Will the cleansed waters bring more mouths to feed than food with which to fill them'. The medical scientist, therefore, backed up by the agricultural scientist, is largely responsible for the rapid increase which is taking place in world population and he can properly be expected to accept a large share of the responsibility for solving the problems which arise from it.

By contrast, there is little evidence that the population explosion is due to an increase in the biological fertility of the human race or even to a real increase in demographic fertility,

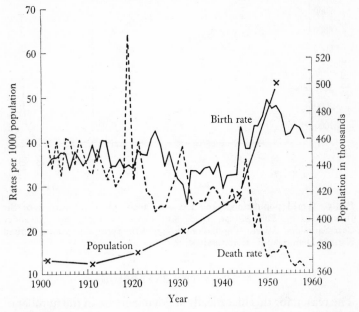

Fig. 6   Mauritius. Birth-rates, death-rates and population, 1901–58. (After R. Titmus and B. Abel-Smith, 1961. *Social Policies and Population Growth*, Methuen.)

that is in birth-rate. This, of course, raises a point of definition. To the biologist, fertility means potential fertility, the ability to produce offspring. To the demographer, it means actual performance. Thus to a demographer, a woman who has had a child, but then for some reason has had her ovaries removed, is a fertile woman. To a biologist this is an odd conception, to say the least, and it has some odd results. I heard it said recently that, on some particular occasion, for reasons of economy, the Registrar General had put questions about their fertility only to women under fifty years of age!

THE FUTURE

In the human race, therefore, the limiting factor of infective disease has been dramatically relaxed over the last half-century and the number of people is rushing upwards. What is likely to happen next? Under natural conditions, the relaxation of one limiting factor allows a population to increase until it bumps up against the same factor again, perhaps in a different form, or against one of the other two factors, and there is little doubt as to which, in our case, the other would be. It is true that the present population explosion could not have happened without a striking increase in food supplies and other resources, but we cannot hope to build them up to a level providing indefinitely an acceptable standard of living for a world population increasing under the explosive force of geometric progression. It is likely, therefore, that in the absence of any other limitation, famine which is always with us in some form in some part of the world, will be intensified.

And here I must interpolate a most significant point. The sudden decrease of the death-rate in areas where birth-rate remains high has resulted in a staggering excess of young people compared with older people. According to a recent statement by the Population Reference Bureau, half the people now living on earth have been born since the end of the Second World War, twenty-two years ago. This global figure, however, is much exceeded in certain areas, where half the population may be under eighteen or even fifteen years of age (see Fig. 7).

There is no need to emphasize the reproductive potential of age distributions of this kind and no foreseeable circumstance, except an atomic war, is going to stop a tremendous increase in world population over the next two decades. In these circumstances it is of vital importance to give urgent attention to accelerating the build up of food supplies and other resources, to cope with the inevitable massive increase in population within the visible future.

Indefinite increase of resources, however, is neither practicable, as indicated above, nor ultimately effective. Even if it could be achieved, and we were able to control new manifestations of infective disease, it seems that we should run into non-infective disease of a kind which is now receiving considerable attention

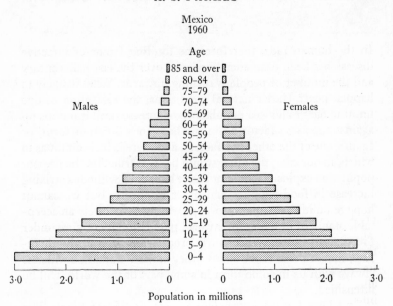

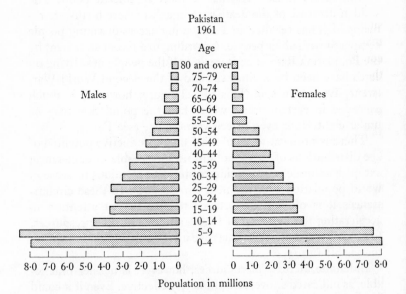

Fig. 7 Population profiles. (After P. Sargant Florence, 1964. *Eugenics Review*, **56**, 143.)

and which may be thought of as a built-in biological control mechanism. Against this background, it is good to see that those concentrating on the provision of food, including organizations such as Oxfam and War-on-Want, on the one hand, and the family planning organizations on the other, are both coming to recognize that the world problem must be tackled at both ends.

I am here reminded of what is said to have been an ancient test for lunacy. The patient was handed a bucket and told to empty a tank which was rapidly being filled with water from a gushing tap. If he turned off the tap before starting work with the bucket he was judged to be sane; if he began to use the bucket without bothering about the tap, he was diagnosed as mad, or, at best, very stupid.

BIOLOGICAL CONTROL MECHANISMS

It is well known that following sudden expansion, animal populations may crash for reasons which have no obvious connection with food supply. Analysis of such crashes, together with a study of experimental situations, has shown pretty clearly that they are due to overcrowding, the physiological results of which are remarkably similar to those stemming from derangement of the hypophysial-adrenal axis. Calhoun's list of abnormal types appearing among rats housed at double the density compatible with a normal population is indeed formidable and includes unmaternal mothers, homosexuals and zombies. Calhoun's experiments are vividly summarized in an article on the 'Cibernetics of Population Control' by Hudson Hoagland who describes yet another category as follows:

The strangest of all of the abnormal male types, described by Calhoun, were what he called the probers. These animals...took no part at all in the status struggle. Nevertheless they were most active of all the males in the experimental population, and they persisted in their activities in spite of attacks by the dominant animals. In addition to being hyperactive, the probers were hypersexual, and in time many of them became cannibalistic. They were always chasing females about, entering their nests, having intercourse with them in the nest – a thing that the normal rats would never do. These probers conducted their pursuits of oestrus females in a very abnormal manner, abandoning all courtship ritual...

So much for the pathology, perhaps we should say the ethological pathology, of over-crowding, or as Calhoun called it 'pathological togetherness', than which there could be no better description of Cambridge on a Saturday afternoon.

The relevance of this to my present theme is well put by Julian Huxley, who, referring to the psycho-physiological stresses arising in animals from over-crowding, says 'This is of immense importance for man too, because in him stress will manifest itself in mental instability and all kinds of social and political disturbance.'

SOCIAL CONTROL MECHANISMS

Biological built-in control mechanisms, however, are not the only possibility. In the past at different times and in different places, man has developed customs and traditions, euphemistically called cultures, which consciously or unconsciously, must have had the effect of retarding population growth—human sacrifice, cannibalism, ritual mutilation of the genitalia, religious persecutions, racial massacres and the immolation of wives, servants or slaves to accompany their master into the next world. One of the gruesome illustrations in von Hagen's book has the legend:

Human hearts were the food of the gods, and without them the world could not continue. When the great temple of Huitzilopochtli was dedicated in 1486, the Aztecs amassed more than 20000 sacrificial victims who lined up, waiting their turn of the knife. Four men hold the victim over a stone, the priest cuts deeply with a flint knife, pulls out the palpitating heart and offers it to the Sun-God. Still warm and quivering, it is deposited in the lap of the recumbent Chac-Mool. The body of the victim is cast down the temple stairway.

Such practices seem to have flourished especially in what is now Latin America. One of the most pathetic sights I have ever seen was the body of an Inca prince, 10 or 12 years old, sacrificed to the Sun-God some 500 years ago, put in an Andean cave above the permanent snow line, there freeze-dried by nature over the centuries, discovered a few years ago and now kept in a glass refrigerator in the museum in Santiago, Chile.

More positive approaches to population control have been not infrequent. The Royal Society Population Study Group was told recently of the Island of Tikopea, in the British Solomon Group, where excess young people were at one time sent out to sea, the males in canoes, the girls to swim. Even the canoists were not likely to reach another island, but nevertheless this seems to have been a gross case of sex discrimination.

Mainly, however, primitive people have relied for population control on infanticide, widely practised in many parts of the world, to reduce numbers or to keep subject peoples in subjection. Hence, among a vast literature, the Biblical legend of Moses hidden in the bulrushes to avoid this fate. Frazer's monumental work *The Golden Bough* is rich in accounts of such methods of population control: for instance, the inhabitants of Rook Island, New Guinea, are recorded as killing the first, third and fifth, etc. children of every woman. The methods of killing, exposure, strangling etc., were as diverse as the fate of the child's body, which might be buried, burned, eaten with religious ceremony or thrown out for the animals.

THE CHOICE

In the world as it is today it seems that we have three possibilities in front of us. (*a*) We can let things rip until the population explosion is stopped by famine, by disease of some sort, by war, which scientists have now for the first time made really efficient for the slaughter of human beings, or by the emergence of built-in biological or social control mechanisms, (*b*) we can rely on a spontaneous decline in human fertility or (*c*) we can take conscious control and make biological history by adjusting our reproductivity to the potentialities of our environment.

CHANGES IN HUMAN FERTILITY

Few people, aware of the implications, can really want to let things rip. What about a spontaneous decline in fertility? Herbert Spencer, in the middle of last century, concluded that 'fertility is proportional to the size and heterogeneity of the species and to the activity and complexity of its life'. He applied this principle particularly to educated and intelligent women whom he seemed to dislike. The modern manifestation of this idea is that of the demographic cycle, which postulates that as standards of living increase, fertility falls automatically and will do so in the East as it has done in the West over the last three-quarters of a century. Accessory to this theory are the ideas that people come to prefer luxuries to babies, and that, if they can be persuaded that most of their children will live, they will naturally have fewer.

This sounds fine, but even if people do decide that they prefer luxuries to babies and do not now need a large number of children to ensure that some grow up, how is this decision to be implemented? Whatever may be happening demographically, potential human fertility remains at a high level. Will it continue to do so? I have pointed out previously that time and money is being lavished simultaneously to remedy the infertility of the infertile and to limit the fertility of the fertile. This paradoxical state of affairs may be justifiable socially but one cannot help wondering where it is leading biologically. Are we in fact so decreasing the survival value of fertility and so increasing the survival value of infertility that we are likely to produce a race of subfertile people, able to propagate themselves only with continuous medical assistance? This might be good for medical business but it would hardly be desirable. Evidently no categorical answer can be given to this question at present but at least we should realize the possible consequence of current trends. I hasten to add that so far there are no signs of such consequences: on the contrary, the indications are that potential human fertility may even be increasing. Certainly, in the West, the length of the reproductive phase of the life-cycle in the female is being increased by the earlier appearance of puberty and the later appearance of the menopause. The acceleration of puberty is not as rapid as is often supposed, but it is still appreciable.

Moreover, the present fashion in the West is for earlier marriages and this means larger families, at the rate, it is said, of one-quarter of a child for every two years earlier marriage. Again, the number of twins arising from a dual ovulation appears to be increasing in some countries. This could be a sign of greater biological fertility. The inevitable conclusion is that the fall in the birth-rate in the West during the last 80 years, associated with raised standards of living or the realization that the children will probably live, must have been due to the conscious limitation of fertility by some means or other. There is no evidence of decreased intercourse, and in the absence of widespread positive contraception the means were presumably *coitus interruptus* and abortion.

COITUS INTERRUPTUS AND ABORTION

As to *coitus interruptus*, I need only say that it is a highly un-reliable but still very common method of attempting to control conception, and that in many cases it amounts to cruelty to the woman, whose reactions at the most significant ages are slower than those of the male, and who is therefore subjected by *coitus interruptus* to a psychotogenic combination of anxiety and frustration.

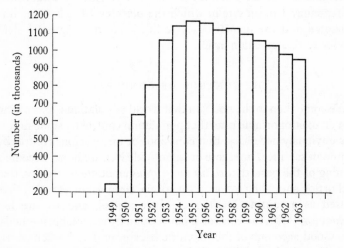

Fig. 8 Japan. Number of induced abortions, 1949–63. (After Pierre Simon 1960. *Le Controle des Naissances.* Petite Biblioteque Payot, Paris.)

As to abortion, I would advocate it without hesitation for emergency use, as in the case of a pregnancy resulting from assault or seduction, or where there is a strong probability of the child being defective in some way, or in serious need as a last resort, but it seems to me to be a poor method for routine birth-control. First, it releases the male from all responsibility and in the long run must surely breed resentment in all but the most docile of women. At meetings I have often been asked, why not simply rely on abortion for birth-control? but the question has always come from a male! Secondly, it is biologically wasteful, since it is usually carried out after the initial physiological changes of pregnancy have happened and the initial disabilities incurred. Thirdly, once established as a recognized method of birth-control it becomes big business with vested interests, and as such may be difficult to replace by contraception. This is well shown by events in Japan (see Fig. 8), which by reason of its small size and good communications might have been thought ideal for the spread of modern contraceptive methods.

But in thus looking askance at abortion as a routine method of birth-control, we must be very clear as to what we mean by abortion. In my opinion the word can apply only to the early termination of an established pregnancy, and by established pregnancy I mean one in which the blastocyst has become implanted and the menstrual cycle has been interrupted. I shall refer to this question again.

THE CONTROL OF CONCEPTION

We come then to the position that world population is increasing at an unsupportable rate, that population control by some means is obviously necessary, that conscious or unconscious control by human sacrifice, massacre or infanticide has, we hope, become a thing of the past, that *coitus interruptus* amounts to cruelty, that abortion should be reserved for special circumstances rather than used as a routine method of birth-control, and we are left therefore, with the control of conception by acceptable methods.

Good accounts of the scientific background and practical use of the pill, the IUCD and the rhythm method are given in the WHO reports and other publications listed among the references. I shall refer here only to some recent findings, of which the first item relates to a striking development in pill technique.

Dr J. M. Manautou in Mexico City has been achieving remarkable results in fertility control by continuous microdosage with one of the orally active progestogens. Such medication does not prevent ovulation and does not give good control of the menstrual cycle. It is, however, very effective in the inhibition of conception. This development is of especial interest to those who have long believed that the great effectiveness of the conventional pill is due at least in part to secondary antifertility factors supplementing the usual but not invariable suppression of ovulation. These supplementary anti-fertility factors were commonly supposed to be changes in the endometrium and changes in the cervical mucus making it impenetrable to spermatozoa. Dr Manautou's work is of particular importance because it is easier to do something every day than to do it on twenty days in twenty-eight and because the great reduction in dosage much decreases both the cost of the medication and the probability of side or long-term effects.

The second item is this. I have spoken on previous occasions of the desirability of developing a technique of fertility control which would act retrospectively in the sense that it could be used in, say, the third week of the cycle to prevent implantation if an egg had been fertilized. Following the demonstration forty years ago that oestrogenic extracts had this effect when given after oestrus in laboratory rodents, the possible applicability of the reaction to man has been discussed many times. But only recently apparently has a really relevant experiment been carried out. I refer to the work of Dr van Wagenen of Yale, who obtained a clear-cut inhibition of pregnancy by the administration of an artificial oestrogen to Rhesus monkeys after ovulation and mating, and to the clinical application of this principle by Morris, also of New Haven.

On the other side of the picture, controversy still rages about the design, effectiveness, side-effects and mechanism of action of the IUCD, and doubt about the mechanism especially is having unfortunate results. In a leading article in *The Times* on 6 January, 1967, it was stated that the intra-uterine device was 'not really a contraceptive, but an abortifacient'. I regard this statement which implies not only that the prevention of implantation is abortion, but that the IUCD acts in that way, as grossly misleading.

I would make three comments: (*a*) Abortion is a ridiculous word to apply to the failure of implantation of a fertilized egg, an event which does not disturb the menstrual cycle, cannot be detected and can only therefore, be hypothetical. As to the argument about destroying human life, I do not propose to go into the question of the stage at which a fertilized egg becomes a human being, except to remark that unless one is going to regard an identical twin as only half a human being with only half a soul, it must presumably be later than the time at which the embryo divides to form identical twins, that is, well after implantation. (*b*) I have repeatedly stated my view that conception means implantation, not fertilization of the egg, and there are good biological grounds for this definition. It follows that contraception can properly be exercised up to the time of implantation, so that even if the IUCD did act by preventing implantation of the fertilized egg it would still be a contraceptive device, not an abortifacient. (c) Evidence as to the mode of action of the IUCD is indeterminate but indications that it acts by preventing fertilization rather than by preventing implantation are not lacking.

Also on the other side of the picture, one must unfortunately record that no progress has yet been made in evolving a safe, effective and acceptable method of fertility control for the male. It seems, therefore, that better methods than those now available will undoubtedly be developed, and in the long run the limiting factor will obviously be motivation to restrict families to a size compatible with an acceptable rate of population growth. What are the chances that such motivation will appear sufficiently soon to have a significant effect before the situation becomes even more critical?

CURRENT EFFECTS OF CONTRACEPTION ON WORLD POPULATION

First of all, are there any signs of an impact on population growth of the existing use of birth-control? For instance, what is going on in the United Kingdom? According to the Annual Report of the Chief Medical Officer of the Ministry of Health for 1965 some half-a-million women in the United Kingdom are now thought to be using the pill. This represents about six or seven per cent of women between twenty and forty-five. The increasing use of the pill in the United Kingdom has been associated with a slight decline in the birth-rate, from 18·5 in 1964 to 18·1 in 1965, and 17·7 in 1966.* No association, however, is necessarily a causal one and the Government Actuary has said that compared with the economic factor the pill has been a small influence in the recent decline in births. Similar declines

Footnote added May, 1968. This lecture was written early in 1967. Pill users in the United Kingdom are now thought to be approaching one million, and the provisional figure for the 1967 United Kingdom birth-rate is 17·2 per thousand. Pill-users throughout the world are now estimated to number around 15 million.

in the United States, Australia and New Zealand are no doubt of equally complex origin, and may well be reversed for equally complex reasons. Taking the world as a whole the situation is not very promising. Only Japan has drastically slashed the birth-rate in the last ten years, and, as already pointed out, this was effected by a crash programme of abortion.

Turning now to global aspects, a recent note issued by the Ford Foundation says 'some 8 or 10 million throughout the world are making effective use of the present generation of oral contraceptives. But the need to take pills 20 days a month under medical supervision together with the cost, make them useful primarily for educated middle classes, a rather small proportion of the world's 600,000,000 women of reproductive age'. In India it is estimated that perhaps 4 million couples are using contraception of some kind or other, that is perhaps five per cent of the total. It would seem therefore that, if the Indian couples using contraception had no children at all there would be a cut of only five per cent in the birth-rate, a negligible figure compared with the aim of 50 per cent. The same is probably true of other parts of the East and of South America, where the biggest increases in population are taking place. It would seem therefore that existing programmes of fertility control can have but little *immediate* effect on the growth of world population, and that a huge extension of the programmes will be necessary. What are the chances of this coming about quickly and effectively? Here we need to consider two factors, (*a*) the opposition, and (*b*) the personal motivation of the individual.

THE OPPOSITION

The opposition is on the retreat but far from overcome. After many millions of words of discussion the Vatican has so far failed to give any formal relaxation of the Catholic Church's stringent dictates on the subject of positive birth-control. I doubt if this is as serious as is commonly supposed. It is likely that the dictates are being honoured more in the breach than in the observance, and sooner or later the hierarchy will have to relax its dogma to save its face. In the meantime, the rest of the human race, the vast majority, which hold different views, should refuse to be intimidated by a small but noisy minority.

National anti-contraception legislation is also disappearing, but the last restrictive State law in the United States was repealed only in 1966, after American organizations had been promoting birth-control programmes in other countries for many years. Canada still has an anti-birth-control law on the Statute Book, and a very curious one it is. Under the title 'offences tending to corrupt morals', the criminal code states: 'Anyone commits an offence who knowingly without lawful justification or excuse offers to sell, advertises, publishes an advertisement of or has for sale or disposal any means, instruction, medicine, drug or article intended or represented as a method of preventing conception or causing abortion or miscarriage'. Nowhere is a justification or excuse defined, and the law as it stands forbids instruction even in the rhythm method. It is not surprising in view of all this that Western contraceptive missionaries in the developing countries sometimes come up against a lingering belief that contraception like charity should start at home.

On the international scene, the International Planned Parenthood Federation has made very rapid strides over the last few years, but it is still a voluntary body with only consultant international status. The World Health Organization for many years was prevented by the obstruction of certain member states, notably Eire, from giving desperately needed help in fertility control to other member states such as India, a fantastic situation when one considers the relative sizes of the populations and the relative importance of the countries concerned. Happily this unfortunate state of affairs has improved somewhat, because the WHO now has a Human Reproduction Unit, one of the duties of which, since 1965, is to collect and collate information about contraception and make it available to member states on request. An attempt in 1966 to obtain a small extension of this modest remit was defeated in the Assembly by what was referred to in the press as a combination of Catholic and Communist states. Organized opposition, however, in the end, may be less serious than the obstruction caused by individuals who, while appearing to give full consideration to the various aspects of the problem, conclude, for reasons which may be more obvious to others than to themselves, that fertility control is unnecessary or unlikely to be effective, or else damn it with faint praise.

In the long run, nevertheless, when ideological and conditioned opposition has finally crumbled man's parental urge may well be a final obstacle, and I turn now to the question of motivation, which in my opinion is going to be the decisive factor.

PERSONAL MOTIVATION

I have pointed out before that the present rate of growth of world population is about two per cent per year, and given good reasons for the view that such a rate of growth is not indefinitely supportable. I have suggested that a rate of 0·5 per cent per year might be acceptable, and that according to published figures such a rate of growth, in the light of present social and medical trends in the West, might correspond to an average family size of around two and a half. The critical question is whether people, even when fully informed of the desirability and practicability of family planning, will wish to restrict their families to this extent in the interests of population control. The answer may well be 'no'. At best, it will be a long time before people are influenced by global population problems in deciding how many children they wish to have, and there will always be some who feel superior and regard it as a duty to produce large families.

In the East and in South America, the immediate problem is to promote the idea of family planning. According to Dr Berelson of the Population Council, this aim is more nearly achieved than might be thought, and progress waits on the development of more simple methods. This may well be optimistic and few would disagree with the view that any widespread practical appreciation of problems of world population will not come quickly. In the meantime, the medical scientist continues to accelerate the growth of world population, the agricultural scientist struggles with the problem of feeding the multitudes, the educationalist fights a losing battle against illiteracy, and the sociologist ponders on the results of increasing miscegenation. The biologist, less emotionally involved, speculates, as I have done today, on how soon the crunch will come.

POPULATION, FOOD SUPPLIES AND ECONOMIC GROWTH

by R. T. F. King

During much of the nineteenth century, economics had a reputation as 'the dismal science.' This was very largely due to the prognostications of economists on the subject of these essays. This reputation was acquired from the widespread acceptance, among the economists now usually described as 'classical' economists, of some of the views of T. R. Malthus. Malthus's *Essay on the Principle of Population* was first published in 1798. Under the pressures of controversy, later editions of the Essay were modified and greatly enlarged, and went through a whole series of revisions. Long and unsystematic, it was easy for the supporting arguments to be misinterpreted and for the name of Malthus to become associated with ideas, such as the promotion of birth-control, that he specifically repudiated. But the Principle itself can be readily summarized: if unchecked, population will tend to increase at the rate of a geometric progression, whereas food output can at best increase at the rate of an arithmetical progression. Therefore population will always tend to outrun available subsistence. Checks to population growth might be those of 'vice, misery or moral restraint.'

Just why food supplies could not increase at some steady growth rate, which might perhaps have been greater than the steady growth rate assumed for population, was not clearly explained by Malthus. But David Ricardo, writing a few years later, made the underlying idea clearer and more plausible. Adding successive units of labour to a fixed supply of land would lead to diminishing increments of output. This is one aspect of the famous 'law of diminishing returns.' So as population rose, average output per man would fall.

At some point, output per man would fall to the minimum level compatible with physical subsistence. Vice and misery would stop population from rising further, but not short of that point.

Only moral restraint could do that. Classical economists differed in their degrees of optimism about the achieving of this moral restraint, but were generally agreed that population growth would increase as incomes rose. Measures such as poor relief were therefore detrimental to economic progress, and would prove self-defeating. Some writers appreciated that a sufficiently rapid rise of the capital stock could modify these arguments. But nevertheless most economists in the first half of the nineteenth century were very pessimistic about the long-term level of wages.

In later decades of the nineteenth century, economic development could be observed to be raising general standards of living in a number of countries. But far from this calling forth a more rapid rate of growth of population, the reverse seemed to be the case, and birth-rates in industrialized countries started to fall. As this happened, economists stopped believing that increases in income would bring forth additional population, at least to the extent that would keep population always pressing against the means of subsistence, although the basic notion has not completely been abandoned. In the interwar years the most pressing economic problem was the high level of unemployment, and the fact that the most developed economies were tending to produce more goods than could be sold and inducing world depression was a much greater worry than whether mankind could feed itself. The apparent imminent reversal of population growth added to anxiety about employment problems. Following the work of J. M. Keynes, however, economists obtained a much more complete understanding of the operations of the economic system and hence of the way in which mass unemployment could be averted. In addition, levels of fertility increased in industrialized countries, and fears about eventual population decline have vanished. In their place has returned the old anxiety about the rate of population growth in the world as a whole in relation to food supplies, and with it, a widespread belief that the present rate of population growth in the poorer countries is a serious impediment to their economic progress in ways quite divorced from the question of food supply. I shall deal first with the possibility that population growth might press increasingly upon subsistence, proving Malthus and his colleagues correct. I shall then discuss the wider economic aspects of population growth.

The views of the classical economists on population and food supply turned out to have been wildly over-pessimistic, or, at the very least, hopelessly premature. They did not foresee the great increases in food output of the last century and a half. This has come partly from the opening up of land to commercial production in the United States Midwest, in Canada, in Argentina, in Australia and in New Zealand. This was a development largely made possible by revolutionary advances in transport— the coming of the railways and the steamship.

The growth in food output was also due to improved agricultural techniques in the more advanced countries. Famines did occur in Europe in the nineteenth century, notably in Russia and in Ireland, but in Northern Europe, at least, there was already enough rise in agricultural output in the second quarter of the century to permit a steady increase in population before the effects of opening up new land overseas had been felt.

The increase in agricultural productivity in the more developed countries of the world is still going on and at a remarkable rate. For example, between 1950 and 1960 output per man in agriculture rose faster than in industry in Denmark, Britain, Canada and the United States, and in all the countries of the European Common Market except Italy. In Britain and the United States it rose about twice as fast, and in Canada even faster. In these countries, agricultural growth has not only been able to keep pace with the rise in population but has also been able to release labour to the other sectors of the economy. Whereas the poorest countries of the world have about 70 to 80 per cent of their labour force engaged in agriculture, a country like the United States can manage to be a major agricultural exporter with only seven or eight per cent of its labour force on farms. Until quite recently the agricultural problems of the wealthy advanced nations of the West increasingly seemed to be how to prevent the acquisition of unsaleable surpluses. These had been accumulating for several years in the United States despite most earnest attempts to control production, and were now threatening Western Europe. Considering the advanced countries as a group, but separately from the world as a whole, the adequacy of food supplies in the foreseeable future is not in doubt.

The increases in agricultural productivity have not, however, been world-wide. In the countries that are poorest today—those in Asia and Africa—productivity has remained at levels passed in Europe several centuries earlier. To some extent, Malthusian checks have remained operative, but improved transport has made possible the reduction of famine. This has reinforced the medical and public health factors in largely disconnecting the death-rate from the level of incomes in the society.

In these countries conscious family limitation or forces making for later marriage have had little impact on birth-rates. So birth-rates of over 40 per thousand combined with death-rates of under 20 per thousand have become the norm, giving a rate of population increase of at least two per cent per year. In some countries in Latin America, population growth-rates have risen as high as four per cent a year. Underdeveloped countries as a group contribute the major part of the increase in world population. They are also by reason of their poverty the first victims of any food crisis.

What would be the probable nature of such a crisis, and how likely are we to have one? This may seem in some ways a senseless question, since have we not already had such a crisis in this decade? To answer these questions it will be helpful to divide into three, the problems of food supply confronting us according to the period of time involved. The first are our contemporary problems; the second, those which are likely to continue or to develop over the remainder of this century; and the third, those which are really long-term problems and raise questions about the eventual carrying-capacity of the earth.

When an economist is asked whether the supply of some commodity will be adequate he must first consider how much of that commodity will be demanded at each different price. Then he will ask about the technological possibilities of producing that commodity, and what it would therefore cost to supply that commodity to those who wanted to buy it. If it appeared that the amount demanded was likely to be greatly in excess of supply at the current price, which might therefore be expected to move very sharply upward, he might then use the words 'shortage' or 'crisis'. In this sense there is no food shortage on a major world-wide scale at the moment. There has been no general tendency for the prices of major foods to rise, except perhaps in the case of rice and then only very recently. It may reasonably be

TABLE 2. *World Cereal Supplies: Production and Stocks*

	Million metric tons				
	1962–3	1963–4	1964–5	1965–6	1966–7
WHEAT					
World production excl. centrally planned countries	151·6	153·5	161·6	160·9	162·9
World production excl. Asian centrally planned countries	236·3	216·7	250·3	239·1	281·2
Stocks at end of year	52·8	44·5	44·2	32·8	35·9
COARSE GRAINS					
World production excl. centrally planned countries	318·8	335·2	322·9	344·9	352·6
World production excl. Asian centrally planned countries	406·4	418·2	422·4	432·7	451·9
Stocks at end of year	64·3	71·2	56·1	45·0	36·9

SOURCE: *FAO Monthly Bulletin of Agricultural Economics &*
Statistics, July/August 1967

objected, however, that a food crisis in the period 1965–7 was avoided only because the world as a whole and the United States in particular ran down stocks, especially of wheat, but also of coarse grains. Stocks of wheat held by major exporters fell from about one-third to one-fifth of the annual output of non-communist countries, and those of coarse grains from about one-fifth to one-tenth. Stocks of wheat are now about the same level as fluctuations of wheat output from one year to another. This is not itself alarming but the comfortable safety margin of stocks of grain built up during the 1950s has disappeared (see Table 2). Stocks of rice are very low and there are indications that demand (at current prices) will tend to grow faster than supply over the next few years.

Looking at the behaviour of food prices and of food output in relation to the demand for food may not seem very satisfactory in view of the low levels of nutrition among many millions of the world's inhabitants. Another approach to the question is to ask how far present levels of nutrition fall below minimum acceptable standards and to use this as a measure of food shortage. Food is one of the few commodities for which it might make sense to talk about human 'needs' or 'requirements', rather than simply ask how much will be demanded at given prices. Nutritional requirements are discussed elsewhere in this book. In practice, and apart from the considerable disagreement among experts about minimum nutritional requirements, it is impossible to estimate what a figure for an average national calorie intake per head might mean in terms of the intake for different groups of the population, in view of the very uneven distribution of income that prevails in most underdeveloped economies. In addition there is the statistical difficulty that, where food is consumed on the farm where it is grown, its volume is difficult to estimate. Available figures of nutritional levels do not therefore lend themselves to precise statements of easy interpretation. It seems safe to say, however, that very large numbers of the population do not get enough to eat in terms of requirements for physical efficiency and good health. In this sense, it might make sense to say that there is a food shortage.

Having said that, however, there is little evidence that the situation has really taken any turn for the worse, and still less that current food deficiencies can be blamed on population growth. Nutritional levels are far from ideal, but this has been so, no doubt, throughout the history of mankind. It is clearly disappointing that endeavours to raise consumption per head have not been more successful, and no doubt population growth has made this a good deal more difficult. At present, however, mankind is accomplishing, rather precariously, the somewhat meagre achievement of maintaining *per capita* food consumption.

The short-run situation is, unfortunately, a little more gloomy than the preceding paragraph might indicate. Food production *per capita* in the underdeveloped countries as a group has not risen as fast as population. Consumption levels have been maintained by a reduction of food exports or an increase of imports (see Table 3).

For some commodities, such as grains, the change has been particularly dramatic. Before the Second World War, Latin America was the largest world exporter of grain, followed by North America, Eastern Europe (including the USSR), Australia, Asia and Africa. Now only the North American and

TABLE 3. *Indices of 'per caput' food production, net trade and supplies in developing regions*

	Average 1953–7	Average 1958–62	Average 1963–6
	Indices, average 1948–52 = 100		
LATIN AMERICA			
Production	103	103	103
Net export	96	96	100
Supplies	104	104	103
FAR EAST*			
Production	108	114	114
Net import	74	177	269
Supplies	108	115	116
NEAR EAST			
Production	111	117	117
Net import	97	278	320
Supplies	111	121	122
AFRICA			
Production	105	106	106
Net export	107	95	87
Supplies	105	107	108
ALL ABOVE REGIONS			
Production	107	111	111
Net export	107	63	44
Supplies	107	113	113

* Excluding China (Mainland) and Japan.
SOURCE: FAO, *The State of Food and Agriculture*, 1967.

Australian countries regularly export grain. Latin American supplies more or less balance demand, and the other developing areas are net importers. Russia is on balance an exporter, but may be a major importer after years of poor harvest, as in 1965, and China has also had to import large quantities of wheat from North America. It is evident that the current situation makes too many of the world's inhabitants dependent on North America for any of them to feel comfortable about it. In the difficult period of 1965–6 the United States was able to provide vital food aid for India, greatly alleviating a very serious crisis out of its existing stocks. It could not do this again on the same scale without producing wheat directly for aid purposes.

The fact that food production in less developed countries has not risen as fast as population growth is not itself necessarily harmful. There is no reason why in the long run these countries may not be importers of food and exporters of other raw materials and manufactured goods. In the present circumstances, however, where typically more than half the labour force is engaged in agriculture, the failure of food production in underdeveloped countries to keep pace with population growth reflects the very low levels of productivity that still remain. Much of the growth of output that has taken place can be attributed to growth in cultivated areas rather than to increases in yield. Table 4 illustrates this for cereal production, where about only one-half of output growth can be attributed to increases in yield.

TABLE 4. *Average annual increase in production of cereals from 1952–6 to 1963–6*

	% Increase in		
	Area	Yields	Production
Latin America	2·56	1·46	4·06
Near East	1·81	0·62	2·45
Far East	1·12	1·83	2·96
Africa	1·62	1·03	2·66
Average	1·49	1·53	3·05

SOURCE: OECD, *The food problem of developing countries*, 1968.

The possibilities for such increases in the future are much smaller than in the past, especially in the Far East. If food production is to rise as fast as population growth in the future, the rate of increase of yield will have to be very much greater than in the past. Looking further ahead to the end of the century—and the second time period that I want to consider—it is therefore not easy to believe that the dependence of the rest of the world on North America for critical items of food is going to be substantially eliminated. By the end of this century, the population of the world will be of the order of twice its level in the mid 1960s, assuming some drop in fertility in underdeveloped countries as incomes rise there, and they become more urban and industrial and follow the pattern of earlier industrializing countries. If the world is just managing now at a nutritionally inadequate level, how is it going to cope with a population twice as large?

3-2

The issues involved are not only technological. We must also ask what the cost of supplying sufficient quantities of food will be, who will bear this cost and through what mechanism will it be borne. The technological possibilities are discussed elsewhere is this volume. In the immediate future, the only country that can easily expand grain output is the United States of America. Wheat acreage has been severely limited there. The acreage under wheat was brought down from 70 million acres between 1948 and 1952 to 45 million in 1963–4—a drop of over one-third. Nevertheless, total production has risen from about 31 million tons to about 35 million. There therefore exists the possibility of a fairly rapid increase in land under wheat cultivation. Presumably it has been the least good land that has been removed from cultivation, and some may have been taken irrevocably out of crop production. Nevertheless, United States production might quite easily be increased by one-third, which would represent an increase of between one-fifth and one-quarter in the volume of wheat traded, though only about five per cent of the volume of wheat produced. Production of rice and other grains has been controlled by US quotas and here too it appears that there would be no technological barriers to fairly rapid expansion. If one adds to these the expected West European wheat surpluses of perhaps four to five million tons, it does seem that from a technological point of view the immediate situation need not be a desperate one.

In the longer run, the hope must come from increased yields. Considering only wheat, there is a very considerable variation in productivity. India produces an average of only 700 lb of wheat per acre, while in North America, average yields have risen to around twice that level, though Canadian yields, in particular, fluctuate markedly, and have been both much higher and much lower than this in recent years. In Britain, average yield in 1963–4 was 3700 lb per acre. Natural conditions may prevent Indian and American yields from reaching British levels, but it is clear that bringing them nearer to this level would entail an enormous increase in output. If we take other crops, such as rice, where Indian yields are only one-quarter of the Japanese, we get a similar picture.

Normally, in economics, we are not particularly interested in yields per acre. Our concern is with output per man. We are concerned with human incomes, not incomes per acre. It is the total income of the North American producer, with his much larger acreage, which makes him a more productive farmer than his British counterpart, who gets a higher income per acre. But when we are interested in the technological possibilities, then it is the output per acre that does concern us. At a price, North American yields per acre could doubtless be raised much nearer Western European levels. If the price of wheat were high enough, wheat land in the United States would become so valuable that raising yields would be the most profitable thing to do.

Beyond this, it is cost that stops the world from a more productive use of land that is at present uncultivable. In the long run, it may become not only technically feasible but economically advisable to irrigate the Sahara. But food will have to be a lot more valuable in terms of earth-moving equipment, pumps and power before that occurs. This is where diminishing returns in increasing agricultural production become important—it may well take proportionally more and more of our resources simply to maintain our *per capita* level of food production.

But knowing that technologically a particular output could be achieved does not provide an indication of the likely or maximum rate of increase of output. This depends on an enormous number of complex factors—the system of land tenure, the provision of extension services, of credit and marketing facilities, the level of investment, the carrying out of research, are only a few. An American study has estimated that a nutritionally adequate diet for the world's population of the year 2000, on fairly conservative assumptions about the size of that population, would be obtainable with known techniques but only with rates of increase of yield equal to those obtained in Europe and North America during the 1950s, coupled with the cultivation of all the land classified by the FAO as 'unused but potentially productive'. Such rates of increase were to be obtained from 1960. Already this decade has fallen behind such a target, and it is clearly over-optimistic.

It appears to be technically feasible to feed the growing population of the world, but, as noted, it may cost more per unit of output to do so, and so food prices may rise. Britain imports about half its food. We may pay these higher prices reluctantly and it may cause us all sorts of short-run balance of payments problems, but we can afford it. We, in other words, will manage to pay the increase in the costs of food. But a country like India will probably not be able to afford to do so. If she has to do so, she may well not be able to import machinery, or key raw materials, and other development would come to a halt. This is because the market prospects for her exports, which consist mainly of tea, jute manufactures and cotton textiles, are so poor.

This illustrates an ironical fact about the present situation. We are talking of a food crisis, but it is a crisis concerning mainly temperate zone foods. Countries that export tea, cocoa, coffee, sugar, bananas, cotton and hard fibres, all face acute competition in world markets, slowly rising demand, and constant, if not falling, prices. These are products for which new sources of supply, particularly in tropical Africa and in Latin America, are constantly being found. These are products for which demand is rising much more slowly than world incomes, and which are often subject to competition from synthetic substitutes. The only long-run solution for such countries is to produce and eventually to export manufactured goods. But when, as all too rarely happens, a country, such as India, finds that it can produce a manufactured good, such as cotton textiles, cheaply enough to export it, it is apt to find tariff barriers or import quotas erected against it. Other underdeveloped countries will be protecting their newly established industries and advanced countries protecting inefficient but long established and politically sensitive industries.

If India cannot pay for her grain imports, and the rest of the world is not prepared to allow millions of Indians to starve, and if it is technically feasible to produce enough grain to feed them, how are such imports to be financed? Since 1954 the United States, and several other countries on a much smaller scale, have had a programme of giving away, or virtually giving away, surplus commodities. In the first ten years of the programme, surplus commodities worth 10000 million dollars were given as aid. Wheat accounted for 45 per cent of the total value.

From the United States point of view, these exports have been costless. The products were surplus in that they remained unsold after every measure the United States Department of Agriculture could devise to hold down production had been tried. The only alternatives were to store the products, which

was expensive, or to destroy them, which was politically un-
thinkable in a hungry world. A new expansion of wheat acreage
would not, however, be costless. At present prices another 10
million tons of wheat would cost about £230 million. Even if this
is doubled to allow for the higher cost of expanding wheat
acreage and the provision of other products, this amount is
less than one per cent of current US Federal Government
spending. Since it is unlikely that other aid-giving countries will
want to spend foreign exchange on American agricultural products for aid, the costs involved would have to be borne by the
US taxpayer. Although the costs involved are by no means
astronomical, at least in the short run, the length of time the
American taxpayer is likely to put up with this is probably
limited. Besides no government would want its food supply to be
controlled by the US Congress.

From the point of view of the recipient country, aid in the
form of food is not an unmixed blessing. In most underdeveloped countries, such aid will allow more people to be put to work,
and the amount of investment that can be carried on without
inflationary consequences can be increased. Without such aid,
agriculture might be a bottleneck preventing the efficient use of
other forms of aid. But since food aid can disrupt both national
and international markets for food, the desirable amount of food
aid must remain a relatively small proportion of total food
consumption. If food imports keep the price of food in the
recipient country low, it is quite possible that food output,
especially for sale, will be lower than otherwise. This is not an
argument for allowing prices to rise to famine level in bad years
in a country like India. But there is some evidence that farmers in
underdeveloped countries, as elsewhere, react positively to
steady, reasonably favourable prices. Carefully planned aid in the
form of food need not lower incomes for local farmers if it leads
to a sufficiently increased output of industrial goods to keep the
ratio between industrial prices and agricultural prices the same.
But such a condition requires extremely tight control over the use
of food aid, as well as very careful planning, and this must keep
the amount of food aid which can be accepted relatively small.

Market disruption may also occur in international markets,
and the countries harmed may also be underdeveloped. Thus
commodity aid must have reduced India's demand for rice from

Burma and Thailand and for cotton from the Sudan and Uganda. Such countries may be no wealthier than the recipient of food aid. In any case, the main source of increased food for underdeveloped countries must be domestic agriculture. Without this, the amounts involved may get so large as to be an impossible burden on taxpayers in advanced countries. Since too, the mass of the population in underdeveloped countries is rural, economic development will have meaning only if it can raise rural standards of life. This can only happen through increased agricultural productivity.

Beyond the end of this century we begin to pass into a science-fiction world in which neither the food that will be eaten nor the manner of producing it will necessarily be the same as today. When considering such a world, the economic problems of raising productivity, or financing output, are usually ignored, and the technological possibilities become all-important. Here the average economist can only watch with amazement while others attempt to define the carrying-capacity of the earth. A recent calculation suggested that on current American standards and type of food consumption, 47000 million people could be supported, and that at current Japanese standards, with Asian standards of timber requirements, the figure could be 157000 million. In the very long run, however, where the only limitation is the rate at which plants will photosynthesize dry matter, the same author argues that the numbers to be supported could be several times this figure, and the full support of one person at twice the minimum food standards could be obtained from the cultivation of about 27 square metres.

Before these achievements become necessary we may, of course, assume that other factors, perhaps the sheer discomfort of congested living, will have brought population growth to an end. It is, however, a matter of concern that there is not yet an indication of what the forces are going to be that will eventually bring to an end population growth in the affluent but densely populated societies of the future. While it is to be expected that fertility in the less developed countries will fall, as has happened in all countries that are now industrial, fertility in the latter countries has risen to levels that are far too high to be maintained indefinitely.

While this book is, of course, concerned with population

growth and food problems, and not with all the other issues arising from population growth, it would be extremely misleading if the impression were given that the economic problems presented by population growth mainly concerned food supplies. I shall therefore say a little about other economic aspects of population growth.

The first concerns the possibility that we might run out of some other natural resource. Any use of minerals, whether for energy or for other uses, depletes an irreplaceable asset which one day will be used up at present rates of consumption. It is likely that all presently known reserves of copper, lead and zinc will be used up by the year 2 000. But other reserves may be found. If not, substitutes for these metals are already known or can be developed. With respect to other minerals, most attempts at estimating supply and demand are optimistic about this century. In the longer run, they meet the difficulty that exploring for new reserves is costly, and may not be undertaken if current reserves appear sufficient to supply the likely market over the next decade or two. It is also impossible to foresee technological advance. World development is not likely to have to stop because of a shortage of some critical resources but as with food, the supplies of some may become more expensive. For others, less efficient substitutes may have to be used.

The second, much more worrying, effect of population growth on economic development is its effect in slowing down the rate of accumulation of capital. The essence of economic progress is the raising of the productivity of labour. By far the most important element in this is the accumulation of capital. By this term, I mean capital in its broadest sense—to include machines, roads, hospitals, engineers and Professors of Agriculture. The use that machines can be in raising productivity is obvious. But trained and educated manpower may be just as much in short supply as machines, and may be as urgently needed as investment in machines if the new machines are to realize their full productive potential.

In the majority of undeveloped countries the stock of capital goods is insufficient to employ the whole labour force productively. Those engaged in farming, work very short hours; a fixed amount of work, carrying bags at railway stations or cleaning shoes in the street occupies a very large number of people.

Increasing the quantity of capital per head means diverting resources from current consumption to investment. What this may mean is that some workers and some machines stop producing consumer goods, such as food and clothes, and start producing machines. Children may spend longer in schools and universities before going out to work. Or, in an agricultural society, it may simply mean that more of this year's crop is left as seed for next year's. This diversion of resources from consumption to investment involves, on the part of both individuals and the government, an act of saving.

It is obvious that the proportion of income saved is likely to be inversely related to income per head. A poor country needs all, or almost all, of its resources, just to consume enough to keep its population alive. Nowadays everybody has heard of the so-called 'vicious circle of poverty'. The poorer a country is, the harder it is to save, the less capital accumulation there will be, the poorer the country will remain and so on. Economists do not like this formulation, since it seems to us highly over-simplified, but there is something in it. Many underdeveloped countries can only devote five to seven per cent of their total output to new capital formation. Most advanced countries invest 12–25 per cent of their total output. This is a very significant difference. As a determinant of different rates of growth between countries capital accumulation is only one factor among many. Very much depends on how savings actually made or potentially available are utilized. Nevertheless, capital accumulation is an essential ingredient of economic development.

The impact of population growth on capital accumulation can be broken down into two components. First, the larger the population, the more resources must be used up in consumption, both simply to subsist, and, at more advanced levels, to maintain any particular standard of living. Absolute size would not matter, of course, if the average productivity of everybody in the labour force were the same, and if the proportion of the labour force to total population were unchanged. But the high birth-rates of the fast-growing countries mean that the proportion of labour force to total population will be smaller than in slow-growing countries. In Mexico, for example, where population growth is now about 3·5 per cent per year, 44·4 per cent of the 1960 population was under the age of fifteen, as compared with 31·2 per cent in the United States and about 25 per cent in most European countries. This high proportion of the population must be fed, clothed and educated, with no immediate return.

From the social point of view, this is clearly detrimental to economic growth. From the viewpoint of an individual family, the effects are more ambiguous. Although more children mean more mouths to feed in their early years, not all their costs to society will be borne by their parents. Education, for example, is likely to be financed out of general taxation. Later in life children mean perhaps less hard work and in old age, better insurance. In countries where the only other refuge in times of trouble is the local money-lender, sons may be a better long-term investment than savings under the mattress. In such circumstances, making knowledge of birth control and the means to it widely available will not automatically bring down the birth-rate. There is some clear evidence of a wish for smaller families in less developed countries, and with improved contraceptive techniques, and a change in government attitudes and the recent institution of family-planning policies in a number of countries, there is hope that this will come about. Nevertheless, the size of family that is desired is still generally larger in underdeveloped economies than in developed ones.

The second impact of a growing population on economic growth is the effect of this growth on the average level of productivity of the labour force. Population growth is likely to reduce the rise in productivity by making a given level of investment resources provide capital goods for a larger number of men. The amount of capital that can be provided for each man is reduced. For example, instead of being able to supply its existing labour force with bulldozers, a country must devote its resources to providing the new labour with spades. This is the most serious obstacle to economic development arising from population growth. It is equally true for advanced as for underdeveloped countries. Every new school that we have to build in Britain means the postponement of something else—the modernization of the transport system, for instance. In the less developed countries, however, the capital stock is already inadequate to equip the labour force with the tools needed for modern techniques and widespread unemployment is common. The growth of population makes this employment problem even more intractable.

Against these disadvantages of population growth, there is one advantage of larger population size, which for some countries may partly counterbalance the disadvantages. It is often cheaper to produce things in a large volume of output than in a small one. Economists have long known that specialization can increase efficiency. A larger population may mean a larger market for certain types of goods, which may make it feasible to produce these domestically. This may make possible the expansion of employment without imposing a strain on the balance of payments, and may reduce dependence on a few, precariously placed, export products. But scale arguments are generally arguments for free international trade rather than for population growth. Not all goods can be imported and it is true that it costs less per head to provide public services, such as education, transport, and electric power, if the economy is densely, rather than sparsely, populated. This is important, however, only if aggregate income is larger with a large population, and this may not be so. In addition the size of the market may depend more on *per capita* income than on aggregate income, and for many goods, subject to economies of scale, like durable consumer goods, relatively few richer people may give a larger market than a mass of poor ones. In any case, the scale advantages are of size, not of a fast rate of growth. It is not inconsistent to argue that a country would be better off if it were larger but that its present rate of population growth is detrimental to its development.

It is sometimes argued that population pressure has historically spurred rather than hindered economic growth, by acting as a stimulus to progress. It offers a high incentive to carry out investment and invent new techniques. A growing population is relatively young and the labour force on average has more recently been trained. A growing labour force makes it easier to move labour out of relatively declining industries into relatively expanding ones. A man is more mobile at the outset of his career, and adjustment to a changing industrial structure is easiest if it can be accomplished by steering school leavers into expanding occupations, allowing declining ones to wither away. These are not unimportant factors, though they tend mostly to act in reducing the disadvantages of population growth, rather than being positive virtues themselves. There is no evidence that, historically, population growth has been a major deterrent to economic growth, so no doubt the disadvantages of population growth have been offset by the greater youth and vigour of the growing population. This sort of argument, however, would seem more applicable to already affluent societies than to developing ones, and more applicable to the difference between no population growth and one per cent population growth than to that between one per cent and three per cent growth. When it comes to the virtues of population growth in a country like India, it is impossible not to believe that population growth is a major barrier to economic advance.

India is extremely poor by world standards. Her *per capita* income is only a little over £25 per year. She has to struggle to raise her level of saving high enough to permit an adequate level of investment, and is finding it ever harder to import the raw materials and capital equipment needed to do this. The larger the labour force, the less can capital equipment per head be increased in any given period. It is already impossible for successive Five Year Plans to make a sizeable reduction in unemployment. By the beginning of 1950, there was already a severe employment problem in Indian agriculture. Nevertheless, the size of the agricultural labour force rose by 33 per cent during the decade.

Food is a major bottleneck to development, and its adequacy a constant threat to economic and political stability. Over the period 1960–1–1966–7 population growth rose about 14 per cent. In 1960–1 foodgrains output was 82 million tons; a similar figure is expected for the year 1966–7. In 1965–6 output was 12 per cent below this figure. Two things are desperately clear. It is impossible for such a situation to continue for many years without Malthusian checks slowing down the rate of population growth. It is also impossible for food aid to make good the 14 per cent drop in *per capita* output year after year. India can only seek to increase her own agricultural output, by the provision of irrigation water, of fertilizers, of extension services and research facilities, and by every other means possible. At every stage in doing this, her population growth of over two per cent a year is a burden to her. India is an extreme case among underdeveloped countries, though an important one. The effects of population growth in other underdeveloped countries are of a similar nature to those of India though less dramatic.

45

This is true, and it needs saying, since its truth is not universally accepted by those in a position to influence population policy in less developed countries. But for those of us who are white, from affluent societies, the truth needs saying tactfully. The following quotation by J. M. Stycos from Edmundo Flores, a leading Mexican economist, is worth taking to heart:

A characteristic of this school (neo-Malthusianism) which is deeply resented by the peoples of underdeveloped countries is that it invariably and single-mindedly proposes the limitation of births. They are concerned about reducing the numbers of Puerto Ricans, Hindus, Negroes, Chinese and Mexicans; or else of certain classes and social groups, like the poor, the working class or the Catholics. But they do not worry, for example, about the increase of Aryans, of Protestants, or of Rotarians.

CHAPTER 4

CATASTROPHES AND RESTRAINTS

by A. Leslie Banks

PESTILENCE AND FAMINE

Human communities have always had the potential for growth that has led to the present population expansion. That so rapid and persistent a rate of increase has not occurred earlier in man's history is due to a combination of circumstances of which premature death was, until recently, one of the most important. In this chapter it is proposed to consider first the effects of famine and pestilence and their control and then the less dramatic but equally important causes of premature death which have become more apparent with the decline of the ancient pattern of disease.

Dr Johnson defined famine in his Dictionary as meaning 'scarcity of food; dearth or distress for want of victuals', and he quoted from Hales' Origin of Mankind to the effect that 'Famines have not been of late observed, partly because of the industry of mankind, partly by those supplies that come by sea to countries in want, but principally by the goodness of God.'

There were many references to famine in the ancient world, especially in the Old Testament, but the most vividly recorded are those of medieval Europe and India. France has been particularly susceptible and the great hospital in Paris, the Hotel Dieu, is said to have been founded about A.D. 650 by Bishop Landry for the relief of famine victims. Between A.D. 970 and 1100 there were sixty famine years in France and in 1418 one-third of the population of Paris is said to have died of starvation. It is also recorded that in 1032–3 human flesh was offered for sale at Tournus, not far from Geneva.

As late as 1778 the French writer Moheau was able to say 'I have seen the people of famine areas go out into the fields to eat the grass, and share the food of the wild animals', but the most vivid description is that of d'Argenson, 'I am at present (Oct. 4th. 1749) on my estate in Touraine. I can see nothing here but frightful destitution. It is no longer a gloomy sense of poverty, it is now utter despair which holds the poor in its grip. Their only desire is to die, and they are no longer breeding.'

England also had its famine years, in 1087, 1251, 1315 and 1335 for example, but the last widespread famine in Western Europe was in 1817, with a recrudescence in Silesia, Ireland and Belgium in 1846–8 when the potato blight was followed by rust which destroyed the rye crop. Russia was afflicted throughout the nineteenth century and in 1911–12, and again in 1921–2 when the after effects of war were combined with two years of drought.

It will not have escaped notice that many of these great famines preceded or followed violent social upheavals, wars and revolutions. They were also associated with epidemic diseases of which two, typhus and relapsing fever, earned the unenviable reputation of 'Famine Fever'.

To get a clear picture of famine on the grand scale it is necessary to turn to India, beginning with the droughts of 1640 to 1655 'through all India and beyond'. The list from thence onwards is too long to quote in detail, but in Bengal in 1770 one-third of the people died; in the North-West Provinces in 1837–8 about 800000 people died; in Bengal and Orissa in 1865–6 a million, followed a year later by half a million deaths in Bombay Madras and Mysore. A similar tragedy was only averted in Bengal in 1874 at the cost of £6 million in relief measures and from that time a portion of the revenue was set aside as a famine relief fund. Rene Sand in the 'Advance to Social Medicine' ascribed the comparative security of India from famine since 1900 to three factors, the extension of the railway system, the development of local crafts and industries and improved administrative and financial machinery.

It is now generally accepted that with improved methods of communication and transportation, together with better facilities for international aid, the traditional picture of acute and deadly famine has disappeared. Unfortunately the same cannot yet be said of the fatal epidemics of disease which so often went hand in hand with it.

The spectres of war, pestilence and famine haunted the ancient world. The term pestilence originally comprised any disease that was epidemic and mortal. 'Plague' might mean any disease of great mortality, but 'The Pest' referred to a particular disease entity under various titles such as pestilential cholera, oriental typhus, septic pestilence and so on. It seems clear that plague as we now know it became firmly established in Europe during the reign of the Emperor Justinian, i.e. between A.D. 527 and 565, and from that time it devastated and depopulated the countryside at frequent intervals. The last great outbreak in England was the 'poor's plague' in 1665, when about 70000 people died in London.

Although a number of diseases with widely differing aetiology were included under the term pestilence it is easy to see how this and famine came to be so closely associated, for there is a kind of 'chicken-and-egg' relationship. The conditions responsible for famine, for example devastation by drought, flood, military action, or disease of plants and animals, led to the overcrowded and insanitary conditions which predisposed to pestilence, while the disruption, depopulation, inertia and fatalism following the latter resulted in failure to sow or harvest.

Plague is a disease with high mortality in which man becomes only secondarily involved, for it primarily affects wild rodents. The vector between them and man is the rat flea conveyed by the domestic rat, but what begins in this way as bubonic plague can develop into pneumonic plague spreading directly from person to person.

It would be difficult to exaggerate the depopulation caused by plague, and one example will suffice. It has been estimated that the Black Death claimed twenty million victims, including about one third of the population of England, between 1346 and 1353. As to the association with famine, writer after writer has described the plague as 'breaking out when the population was suffering most from famine', and when the physical and mental misery resulting from destitution was greatest. Even today it is not yet wholly clear, in spite of close research, why plague had disappeared from Europe by the middle of the nineteenth century. In the second half of that century and the early years of the twentieth there was another pandemic, which is believed to have started in the uplands of South-East Asia and which spread by maritime traffic from Chinese ports to many parts of the world. An indication of the declining influence of plague as a regulator of population is that between 1919 and 1956 the average yearly number of deaths reported to the World Health Organization declined from approximately 170000 to less than 200.

Typhus and relapsing fevers, the 'famine fevers', are conveyed from man to man by means of lice, fleas, ticks and mites. Louse-borne typhus is one of the oldest known diseases, with many names, including 'gaol fever', 'ship fever', and 'malignant fever'. It affects especially young and middle-aged adults, with a high mortality and it is, above all, a disease associated with war, poverty and famine. It is associated with war because of the overcrowding of troops in inadequate premises without facilities for cleanliness and with poverty and famine because want and misery, mental depression, overcrowding and dirt go hand in hand. Typhus has traditionally followed defeated armies like a shadow, as in the retreat of the Grand Army from Russia. For centuries it afflicted the poorest areas of Europe, Russia, Poland, Silesia and Ireland. Virchow, the great nineteenth-century pathologist, described Ireland as 'Das Land des Hungers, des Fleckfiebers und des Auswanderung,' hunger, fever and emigration. Fortunately that period belongs to the past and today, no matter how severe the related social conditions might be, typhus can be prevented and controlled. In passing, it may be noted that the medical profession has had a peculiarly personal interest in typhus, for it caused a high mortality among the doctors called upon to treat it. It was this disease, also, which was responsible for the 'Black Assizes', such as that in Cambridge in 1522, when many of the judges and lawyers and local notables died of typhus contracted from the inmates of the gaol brought before them for trial.

MALNUTRITION AND DISEASE

There are many other infectious diseases which occur in epidemic form with a high mortality. As Winslow, the great American epidemiologist, said when discussing scourges of the past, 'Cholera, typhoid fever, malaria and yellow fever have worked havoc on the North American continent within the memories of those now living. All of them...are still vital problems in many parts of the world. None of these maladies—except perhaps yellow fever—have, however, caused such intensive and deadly epidemics or aroused such universal terror as bubonic plague and typhus fever.'

Cholera requires special mention. Known since the days of Hippocrates, every outbreak has been traced back to the Far East, and it is spread by the contamination of food and drink by human excreta. It travels with the speed of man and the mortality is high. With the other 'water-borne' diseases, the enteric fevers and the dysenteries, cholera has been one of the principal regulators of numbers.

Great and fatal epidemics are becoming rare, and modern methods of control are so effective that they are unlikely to return unless there is a wide-spread breakdown of communications amounting, in effect, to a return to the primitive conditions which formerly gave rise to them. Such a possibility is remote, short of total war, but one of the results of the decline of famine and pestilence is that the importance of other killing and disabling conditions becomes manifest. Smallpox, for instance, has been recognized as a major killing disease since it was first described by Rhazes, in Persia, more than a thousand years ago. During the eighteenth and early nineteenth centuries it became one of the principal epidemic diseases of the western world and even today, nearly 200 years after Jenner's discovery of control by vaccination, smallpox claims many thousands of victims each year in the developing countries.

The influence of malaria has been, and remains, even more important for it is not only a major cause of premature death but the chronic ill-health that it produces has profound effects on the growth of populations and on food production. The 'silent' nature of the disease and its lack of dramatic symptoms puts it in a similar category to the other diseases caused by parasitic infestations, such as bilharzia and hookworm. The people chiefly affected do not recognize their serious nature nor can they afford the time for prolonged courses of treatment. Control and eradication of such diseases may require a considerable degree of organization and involve national and international action over large areas. When successful the effect in reducing death-rates can be quite sudden and dramatic.

The 'captain of the men of death' is, however, tuberculosis. This disease reached a dominant position in Europe in the eighteenth and nineteenth centuries and has only been brought effectively under control in the past fifty years. It continues to maintain an iron grip on the peoples of the developing countries,

both in the slums of the rapidly growing cities and in the rural areas. Tuberculosis and the venereal diseases present the greatest problems of control, for the measures required are social rather than medical. The means of prevention and cure are known, but the action required to break up the 'hard core' from which infection is spread is complex and costly.

It is not always appreciated that many of the so-called 'tropical' diseases were at one time common also to the temperate zones. It is not merely a matter of a harsh physical environment, but of a combination of this with poverty, ignorance, bad housing, and faulty customs, habits and beliefs. Control of the great killing diseases by modern methods does not solve these basic factors, but may merely make it possible for more people to live longer under the same or worse conditions than before, with malnutrition and related disease in place of famine and pestilence.

In this context the term malnutrition is used to imply 'ill or badly nourished' and it thus includes under-nutrition as well as abnormal conditions arising from lack of a balanced diet. It need hardly be added that disease may be either a cause or effect of malnutrition. The picture may therefore vary considerably, from starvation due simply to lack of calories to the specific symptoms and signs of a deficiency of one constituent of the diet, as in scurvy resulting from a lack of vitamin C.

Most commonly the manifestations, particularly in children, are those resulting from multiple deficiencies, complicated by associated disease, especially of the gastro-intestinal tract, interfering with the absorption of nutrients. Infestation with parasitic worms should also be noted here, for these have, as it were, first call on the nutrients. Thus hookworm is closely associated with severe anaemia especially among women and children. Heavy worm infestations also contribute to the picture of lethargy and lack of initiative. It is also necessary to bear in mind the possibility of advanced tuberculosis or other wasting disease.

Of recent years an ominous body of evidence has been accumulated to show that in certain parts of the world large numbers of children are suffering from chronic malnutrition and above all protein malnutrition. Poor maternal nutrition may predispose to such conditions as stillbirths and premature births but, in general, the child before birth 'takes what he needs' at the expense of the mother no matter how ill-nourished she may be, and after birth she has to be very ill before breast-feeding fails. The infant may thus be reasonably well provided for in the early months of life, but from the first year onwards the child requires more food in proportion to weight than an adult and about three times as much high-quality protein. If he does not get it he becomes ill and may die. The comparison of death-rates in developing and advanced countries illustrates this well. Whereas the mortality of infants under one year may be ten times greater, the rate among children from one to four years of age may be as much as forty times more.

Due to the combination of malnutrition and disease the manifestations of malnutrition may be indirect, as when an infant dies of an apparently unrelated condition, such as bronchopneumonia or gastro-enteritis, which is the end result of a chain of events of which the primary cause was deficiency of essential components in the diet.

This may be the course of events in the condition known as marasmus seen in infants in the first year of life and characterized by wasted limbs, emaciated body and wizened features. This condition may be due to extreme deficiency of food or to impaired absorption of nutrients by reason of disease and especially severe diarrhoea. More ominous, because of its insidious outset, is the 'sickness of the displaced child', a severe form of malnutrition caused by marked deficiency of protein although there may be quite a high intake of starchy foods.

Many local names have been given to this disease, of which 'kwashiorkor' is the most expressive. The word comes from the Ga dialect of West Africa and means literally 'first-second', that is the disease the first child gets when the second is expected. It may also mean 'red-boy', a reference to changes in colour of the skin and hair in this disease. This unusual word has the advantage of drawing attention to a serious disease of young children which over the past twenty years has been found to be widespread in Asia, tropical Africa and Middle and South America. Although the manifestations may vary from place to place all are due primarily to protein malnutrition.

The onset of the disease is usually after weaning, i.e. between the first and third years, and it is almost entirely confined to those under five years of age. In the early stages the child is not obviously ill but there is loss of appetite, failure to gain weight, and intense misery. These symptoms are followed by swelling of the legs and hands, skin lesions and changes in colour and texture of the hair. As the condition progresses there is almost invariably damage to the liver, and advanced cases die if untreated. There is little resistance to infectious diseases and a high mortality from these is found in areas where protein malnutrition is common. Even in mild cases physical and mental development are often retarded and this damage may be permanent.

The basic causes of protein deficiency in young children are lack of suitable food, or failure to use available food properly by reason of disease, ignorance, poverty, and local beliefs. Examples of traditional prohibitions will come readily to mind, but a new one is rapidly becoming widespread. As a result of increasing contact with the more sophisticated parts of the world the feeding bottle is becoming a status symbol in developing countries, denoting superiority over the 'vulgar peasant' practice of breast feeding. There is also a belief that bought milk is a superior food.

Unfortunately artificial infant foods are usually too costly for the people concerned, so that they are either not purchased or they are used inadequately. Moreover if they are used they may be improperly prepared because of the lack of knowledge or utensils, or the pollution of the local water supply. Locally grown starchy foods are often given instead, or the child has literally to take 'pot luck' with the rest of the family.

Other deficiency conditions in children include blindness, rickets, infantile beri-beri in some rice-eating countries, iron-deficiency anaemia, and the multiple manifestations of lack of iodine including endemic goitre, cretinism, deaf-mutism and mental retardation.

Behind all these conditions is the vicious circle of malnutrition predisposing to infection and of infection aggravating malnutrition. Much of the lethargy, lack of drive and 'fatalism' in under-privileged societies is due to this combination of malnutrition and disease. A varied staple diet with an adequate amount of protein will, of itself, remedy malnutrition, and the mortality of kwashiorkor can be cut by four-fifths with appropriate treatment. It is difficult to visualize the true extent of malnutrition. FAO in the Third World Food Survey estimated that some 300 to 500 million people were actually hungry and underfed, with resulting physical and behavioural abnormalities, as shown *inter alia* by weight loss, irritability, loss of moral standards and lowered resistance to disease.

In passing, it may be noted that there is also an impressive list of conditions associated with over-nutrition, and that war-time rationing in the First and Second World Wars resulted in a decline in diseases associated with high living standards. It has also been suggested that under-nutrition may have played a part in natural selection, in that children with certain hereditary defects failed to live to the reproductive age.

THE PAST HUNDRED YEARS

It is worth considering, at this stage, whether there are any precedents for future guidance. The last period of serious and widespread deprivation in Great Britain was in the 'hungry forties', but as recently as one hundred years ago conditions were still harsh. In 1867 the population of 'England' (i.e. England and Wales) was estimated at 21·5 millions. The price of wheat and potatoes was high and the 'returns of pauperism' showed nearly a million people on poor relief. Emigrants were leaving the shores of the United Kingdom at the rate of over 500 people a day, Irish, English and Scottish in that order. Emigration was 'considerably promoted by the sums annually remitted by residents in North America, either in the form of prepaid passage orders or in cash, to their friends in the United Kingdom'. The sum of £543000 was thus remitted in 1867.

The emigration tables in the twenty-eighth report of the Emigration Commissioners, quoted by the Registrar General in his report for 1867, showed that the total of emigration from the United Kingdom had risen steadily from 2000 in the year 1815 to just under 200000 in 1867, with high peaks in 1832, 1841 and 1842, and 1846 to 1855. The figures included Irish, Scotch [*sic*] and a small number of 'Foreigners'. The occupation of the emigrants in 1867 is interesting, with 'general labourers' most numerous, professional men and farmers next, then miners and quarrymen and other skilled craftsmen.

In spite of the hard times the national birth-rate of 35·9 was the highest recorded since registration had begun thirty years earlier. This rate is comparable with that of many developing countries today. The death rate in 1867, unlike the previous year when there had been a cholera epidemic, was the lowest for five years at 22 per 1000. The average 'mean lifetime' was forty-one years, but this included 'gentlemen' and the professional classes and the average expectation of life from birth of the artisan and the unskilled labourer was very much less. The brunt of the premature deaths fell on the children under five years of age, but childbirth accounted for 3 600 maternal deaths in that year and these did not include deaths from conditions associated with pregnancy.

It is difficult to visualize the scale on which deaths occurred in children and young people at that time. 1867 was not an 'epidemic' year in England and Wales but even so scarlet fever, diphtheria, whooping cough and measles combined to produce a total of over 33 000 deaths. There were some 17 000 deaths from typhus, 2 500 deaths from smallpox, 20 000 deaths from 'diarrhoea' and nearly 1 000 deaths from cholera. Ague (malaria) caused 121 deaths. Bronchitis was the recorded cause of over 40 000 deaths and towering above them all, as it does elsewhere today, was 'Phthisis' (pulmonary tuberculosis) which caused 55 000 deaths, 9 000 of them in London. There were 10 000 premature births, and 'want of breast milk' was the certified cause of some 1 500 deaths.

The great medical statistician, Dr William Farr, in his 'Letter to the Registrar General on the Causes of Death in England for the Year 1867' was much concerned with the fact that 'the births of the present day suffice to sustain a population much larger than the population existing; and yet the births might be increased by one third, as will be evident when it is considered that more than two million women of the age 15–55 are unmarried'. After considering the various possibilities he came to the conclusion that 'to dread, therefore, any ill consequences from arresting epidemics, or to argue on *a priori* grounds that it is impossible in opposition to nature to save life, to prolong life, to strengthen, and in every respect to improve the English race, is illogical; for give them health, and if the increased numbers cannot be sustained on subsistence by their industry within the shores of those islands, the births will naturally decline; but the natural remedies are increased industry to command produce from abroad, and emigration to seek after subsistence on the vast trans-oceanic territories...We have, therefore, everything to hope and nothing to dread from measures of public health and of public safety.'

The lack of education also caused some concern to the Registrar. 'The number who do not write, estimated by the standard of 1867, is 1 182 249. When we consider that many who write their names can scarcely read, and know little of the elements of arithmetic, to say nothing of any other learning, it becomes a question whether the country ought not to make a strenuous effort to educate this great mass of the youthful adult population.'

The 'strenuous effort' began with the compulsory education of children in 1870. From that year, for various reasons, the birth-rate began to fall and by 1929, before the deliberate adoption of contraceptives had become widespread, it had fallen by 60 per cent. Today it is almost exactly half that of 100 years ago. Death rates fell more slowly, but they also are now only half those of that time. On the other hand the population has more than doubled, from 21·5 million to approximately 48 million, and the standard of nutrition is such that the number of malnourished children now reported by the school medical service is negligible. The great killing diseases of early life have been brought under control, including tuberculosis, and the expectation of life from birth is now of the order of seventy years for males and seventy-four for females.

PROBLEMS OF DEVELOPING COUNTRIES

In many developing countries the attack on the adverse human environment has hardly begun and the 'Sanitary Idea' of our Victorian forebears, with its insistence on improved quality and quantity of water supplies, better housing and the abatement of overcrowding, the proper disposal of wastes, the supervision of the quality of food, improved working conditions and so on, has not yet been universally accepted. Instead the order of events is being reversed in some parts of the world, so that the latest medical advances are being introduced on a massive scale to people who are still living within their ancient traditions. Immunization and vaccination, the sulpha drugs, the antibiotics and the insecticides, are suddenly and drastically reducing death-rates while birth-rates remain at their previous high levels.

Meanwhile the lives of the people concerned, their customs, habits and beliefs, their family and social structures, may have undergone relatively little change. To this already unstable situation a new factor, the deliberate control of the numbers of births, is being introduced by new techniques the rationale of which they do not understand and some of which are still under trial in the developed countries.

Now it is one thing for literate societies to adopt 'family planning' on a personal and voluntary basis after full discussion, but it is quite a different matter to introduce 'population control' on a large scale in underdeveloped and developing countries. Even the methods may have to be different. In illiterate societies the regular taking of a pill may be impracticable and the insertion of an intra-uterine device becomes necessary, aided perhaps by the sterilization of the males, and this in areas where there may as yet be no basic medical services adequate to ensure that these methods are effectively supervised. Where such services exist they are commonly overburdened with the prevention and cure of the great mass of disease and malnutrition.

In spite of the sense of urgency it is necessary to ask what the remote effects of these new and powerful advances may be. They do not, of themselves, alter the traditional ways of life or methods of food production. There is another danger also. If these methods of mass control of disease and population appear to be accepted and in general use (appearances can be deceptive especially among rural peoples), a sense of false security may develop. The impression is given that all that needed to be done has been done. But human beings do not always behave like that. Jenner discovered vaccination against smallpox in 1796, but belief in the supernatural origin of smallpox is still widespread, massive outbreaks occur, and it is endemic in many of the areas now under discussion, even in countries where vaccination is 'compulsory'.

It is also necessary to look beyond any immediate success. No society has, as yet, succeeded in stopping voluntarily its growth or even wished to do so. In England and Wales the annual increase is of the order of 0·8 per cent, with nearly 400 000 more people each year. In Japan, by the most determined efforts, the annual rate of expansion has been reduced to one per cent, but that still represents an addition of nearly one million each year.

To expect less developed countries to cut back rates of growth of three or more per cent per annum to one per cent or less is asking a very great deal, especially in continents and subcontinents of three to four hundred million people. For a long time to come there will still be the vicious circle of poverty, malnutrition and disease, physical and mental inertia, low productivity and poverty. The need for more efficient production of food and for the improvement of health will remain. Failure to do so will not result in famine and pestilence but in the lack of will or desire or energy to remedy matters.

One thing is quite clear. The necessary drive and leadership required to break this vicious circle must come from within. Although action can be stimulated by foreign intervention or international action, leadership cannot be artificially created, for it depends on the willingness of the people to accept it even at the expense of changing their ways of life. Any attempt for example, to stop the enormous wastage of food supplies by animals in India, variously estimated at from 10 to 40 per cent, could only be done with the cooperation of the people, for the causes are deeply rooted in their cultural and religious beliefs.

The problems also vary considerably from region to region. In some areas, for example, there are adequate natural resources still to be exploited, while elsewhere lack of water is a major limiting factor. In many rural areas, handicapped by illiteracy and poverty, the introduction of modern concepts of health, adequate nutrition and optimum numbers is going to take a long time.

Obviously a balance must be struck between the numbers of the people to be fed and the amounts of food available, but this is not the simple mathematical exercise that many people would like it to be. It will be decided by the men and women who build up the family units of which a given society is composed. If, for example, it is accepted by the wealthy and literate members that an average of four children comprises the family pattern to which they are willing to conform then the average will rise (or fall) to that level, with the poor and illiterate sections of society following their example after a considerable time lag.

The danger is that panic or punitive measures may be introduced by governments under pressure. It is necessary therefore to set down clearly the basic requirements for successful action. The first essential is that the plans should be realistic for the country or region concerned. Secondly the basic services, including health services, must be available, adequate, and readily accessible. Finally the people concerned must have a sufficient standard of education to understand what is needed and to ensure their cooperation.

CHAPTER 5

MAN'S DIETARY NEEDS

by K. J. Carpenter

It is evident that the number of mouths to be fed in the world will increase rapidly for the rest of this century and beyond. Food production must be increased more than proportionately if the standard of nutrition of these people is to be any better than the standard we now achieve. This is partly a matter of increased agricultural production. It is partly also a matter of improved use of the supplies on which we now rely, and resourceful substitution where advancing biochemical knowledge makes the synthesis of essential dietary components possible.

In this situation it is particularly important that the massive evidence now available on human dietary needs should be widely known and well understood. This evidence has been accumulated over a long period in Universities and Research Institutes. I will take two examples from Cambridge. First, at the beginning of the century it was accepted that a balanced diet needed to contain mineral salts, proteins (the nitrogenous organic material that forms the working tissues of the body) and 'energy' foods, i.e. chemicals that could be combusted in the body to provide energy for work and for chemical synthesis. Sir Frederick Hopkins, the first Professor of Biochemistry in Cambridge, was one of the pre-1914 pioneers who had a feeling that this was not the whole truth. His careful rat-feeding experiments, carried out in make-shift accommodation, made up part of the pattern of knowledge that led eventually to the recognition of a further class of nutrient, the vitamins, organic substances needed only in a few parts per million in the diet, but vital to health. This in turn led to rational measures for the prevention of several diseases which were then recognized as vitamin deficiency states; also to the chemical synthesis and finally the commercial production of several of the vitamins.

Secondly, between the two World Wars, the dramatic developments in the knowledge of vitamins distorted nutritional perspectives in the other direction and it became almost a new dogma that consumption of any food processed by milling or refining so that it had lost part of its vitamins was conducive to a deterioration in health. In 1946 a team, led by Professor McCance and Dr Widdowson, went from Cambridge to study the relative values of white bread and wholemeal bread in supplementing the meagre post-war rations in two German orphanages. The most scrupulous studies showed no difference in the growth or health of the children on the two regimes; both diets, despite having very little milk or meat in them supported very good growth and good health. However, they were rich in green vegetables.

One moral to be drawn from this and from much other work of the period is that there is no one 'right' pattern for a good diet. Many quite different combinations of foods can be used—combinations including individual foods that are, taken by themselves quite unbalanced (white bread is one example, farmhouse butter is another). With chemical analyses of foods, balanced combinations can be worked out in a systematic manner and construction of diets can be much more flexible than with traditional, 'rule of thumb' procedures. Thus, a housewife in Britain is wise to feel that she should serve her family a dish containing milk and a green vegetable every day; but it would not be equally sensible to teach Eskimo women that they must do the same thing. Nutritional aims can be achieved more economically in other ways there, where the relative costs and availabilities of foods are different.

The central finding from all the experimental work in nutrition is that for a diet to be adequate it must contain sufficient quantities of about forty different chemical substances, and that only one of these needs to be deficient for the remainder (in whatever amount they are present) to be inadequate to support health. Conversely, excesses of individual nutrients apparently confer no benefit. Some are clearly needed at less than a thousandth, even a millionth the level of others, though there are still difficulties in deciding exactly what are the minimum quantities of each substance required for a balanced human diet.

MINERALS

The most obvious nutritional requirements, since we cannot convert one atom to another in our bodies, are for the elements themselves, and I have chosen a mineral to illustrate the problem involved in making precise estimates of dietary needs. One used to see in Children's Encyclopaedias the composition of a man broken down into so many buckets of water, enough iron to make two nails, smaller quantities of copper, zinc, magnesium, iodine and so on. But the biggest mineral ingredient, that makes up nearly two per cent of our body weight, is calcium, the metal that forms salts such as chalk (calcium carbonate) or the phosphate salts which make up most of the mineral part of bone.

Clearly if there are no calcium salts in the diet of a child, it cannot continue to grow normally; this is commonsense. The finding that seems contrary to commonsense is that children need much more calcium than they lay down in their tissue and that even fully grown adults also continue to need calcium. In fact the combined daily requirement for the world's adults is many times that of the children. This is due to our being in a much more dynamic state than one might suppose. For example, we may feel that we are the same person that we were four or five years ago but, in fact, materially we are almost entirely different—each brick of our framework having been taken out and replaced. In this process of continual breakdown and replacement a considerable fraction of the material is lost by excretion.

Now, a diet is only adequate in calcium content if it allows tissues to retain the quantities of this mineral that they require for normal functioning. One cannot measure the calcium content of a man directly but one can measure changes indirectly by a 'balance' experiment in which the determined loss by excretion is subtracted from the calculated intake of calcium in the food and water. In experiments with medical student volunteers, whose habitual diet included approximately 0·8 g of calcium per day, it has been found that giving them appreciably less results in their excreting more than they consume, i.e. in their going into a 'negative' balance. This is a part of the evidence that has led to the United States and United Kingdom standards of recommended dietary allowances for such a man being set at the level of 0·8 g per day.

However, critics have pointed out that this is really no evidence at all. A range of different rates of intake could lead to different equilibrium positions. As the intake is increased from one equilibrium, the level of body stores will rise at first until the increased concentration in the tissues is such that the rate of outflow increases to equal the intake. Similarly, a return to the original rate of intake will result in a temporary negative balance, until the body stocks have fallen to their original level. In fact the evidence is that increasing the dietary level of calcium does give this type of response, i.e. a high body content of calcium (stored presumably as a reserve) and, whatever the habitual level, a drop back results in a negative balance for some weeks thereafter. To put it another way, the only true conclusion from a short-term balance experiment is whether the experimental diet contributed more or less calcium than the subject's habitual diet.

Anthropological studies are another source of information. There is no doubt at all that men and women of fine physique live on daily diets containing as little as 0·3 g of calcium in South Africa and South America. They have normal calcium levels in their bones, and teeth actually much healthier than those of the average Westerner. These observations are politically inconvenient. It is very difficult for the United Nations committee of experts to recommend lower standards for non-Europeans than for Europeans. Furthermore, representatives of the dairy industry in the United States (where milk provides much of the dietary calcium) complain bitterly at any suggestion of lowering the nutritional standards there just because of results coming from quite different and less developed cultures with a shorter expectation of life. Yet, equally it would seem ridiculous to propose international standards that could only be reached by distributing calcium supplements to peoples who show no sign of a deficiency of the element.

In fact, the decision of the United Nations' Food and Agricultural Organization (FAO) has been to adopt a compromise standard of 0·45 g per day (see Table 5). To this is added a proviso that where people have become accustomed to a higher intake the consequences of a sudden lowering are not yet understood so that this cannot be recommended. As stated as long ago as 1931 in a League of Nations report on dietary requirements: 'the answers given by the scientists have been numerous and varied. This circumstance has been a matter of amusement at times to the layman, but a source of anxiety and difficulty to the medical men and administrators'. Certainly we cannot hastily condemn a national diet as being inadequate just by comparison with standards that may have been drawn up with different conditions in mind. Yet there are as a result, curious inconsistencies in international tables of recommended dietary standards (see Table 5).

TABLE 5. *Some comparative daily dietary standards for 25-year-old males*

Origin	(Assumed body weight, kg)	Calcium, g	Vitamin C, mg	Calories	Protein, g
USA	(70)	0·8	70	2 900	70
UK	(65)	0·8	20	3 000	91
FAO*	(65)	0·45	—	3 200	43

* Food and Agriculture Organization of the United Nations.

In the particular example of minerals, there is in any case no problem of supply for the increasing world population. In practice, deficiencies are rare. Where there is a risk of deficiency, the problem is an educational one of persuading people to change their diet, or the technical one of finding some way for the diet to be supplemented without the public having to change their habits, For example, the British Government has for many years compelled millers to add a supplement of chalk to wheat flour as a precaution against marginal calcium deficiency in a part of our population.

VITAMINS

Here again, the problem is one of recognition of need and then of dietary education rather than of any real world shortage of vitamins for an expanding population. There are thirteen vitamins known to be required by man. Each is an organic compound which the body needs but cannot make for itself. We normally obtain adequate quantities from our diet because plants and micro-organisms need the same compounds and they do manufacture them for themselves.

To take a single example, vitamin C, also called ascorbic acid, is abundant in many fruits but is deficient in grains and in most of the other dry foods that store well and are invaluable for getting through a Northern winter or, for that matter, for transportation in bulk to a famine area. Scurvy, which is the condition of vitamin C deficiency and is characterized by sores that will not heal and general weakness, used to be a hazard for North Europeans and particularly for sailors. Today it is extremely rare, and this can be explained by changes in the typical diet— more potatoes, green vegetables and fresh fruit or fruit juice. The vitamin can be destroyed by processing of foods, but on the other hand, it can also be synthesized at a moderate cost. In the case of proprietary blackcurrant drinks, for instance, the currants lose their natural vitamin during the storage in preservative before the juice is extracted at the factory, but the synthetic vitamin is added in its place. Thus the housewife's association of flavour and appearance with nutritional value is maintained, and no one is the worse for it, so far as we know, provided that the supplementation is properly controlled. Margarine is an analogous example; the yellow colouring to imitate the appearance of butter must, by law, be accompanied by sufficient vitamin A and vitamin D to equal their levels in butter also.

As with minerals there is great difficulty in fixing an exact 'requirement' figure. One cannot attempt to use a balance experiment since vitamins are partly broken down in the body and lost. It is, of course, relatively easy to assess the intake of vitamin C, for example, amongst communities that remain free from scurvy, and at the other extreme to calculate approximately what must have been the intakes of people who have developed scurvy under special conditions in besieged cities, polar expeditions etc. However, this only gives two groups of figure—the first probably well above requirements, the second well below it. There are wide differences between standards, as is seen again in Table 5. The interested reader should consult Davidson & Passmore for a further account of these problems.

The isolation, identification, and synthesis of vitamins has been a major achievement in food science. Chemical synthesis is now economic in some cases since the amounts required are small. In consequence, synthetic vitamins now have an important place in the nutrition of advanced industrial communities. It is important to recognize that the quantities of vitamins required are small, and are not reduced when the synthetic product replaces the natural. This is not the first step to replacing a bulky natural food supply by a concentrated small volume, synthetic feed.

The great bulk of the food we eat is required first for the energy and secondly for the protein that it contributes. There is no evidence that giving very high levels of vitamins has any effect in reducing the requirements for the major nutrients. It seems rather that we can, with few exceptions, compare our requirements to a chain of individual nutrients; the strength of the chain is the strength of its weakest link, and increasing the strength of other links is irrelevant.

ENERGY

An average man in Britain produces about 3 000 kcal of heat per day. These are kilocalories, or Calories (spelt with a large 'C'), the unit of heat needed to raise the temperature of one kilogram of water by 1 °C. This means that our daily heat output is that needed to raise 30 Kg (or 30 l) of water through the 100° from freezing point to boiling point. The common grains supply approximately 3·5 kcal of usable energy per g. Thus, we would need nearly 1 Kg or 2 lb of wheat or rice per day to obtain all our energy requirement from these sources.

Even a starving, resting man continues to produce heat but at a lower, basal metabolic rate, equivalent on average to about 1 500 kcal per 24 hr. Eating itself is followed by some increase, but physical work is the factor that increases it greatly.

In this country we are, of course, used mainly to conditions where heat is welcome and we have to take positive steps to keep ourselves warm. Some adjustment in calorie standards should be applied in the hot countries, which are also the ones where food problems are acute. There is some evidence that the basal metabolic rate is slightly less in hotter climates and the FAO standards drop by five per cent for a 10° rise in average environmental temperature. In addition, metabolism is also related to body size and adjustments can be made for this. The age structure has a double effect; children need less but so do the older adults.

The allowances made for these factors are set out in Table 6.

TABLE 6. *FAO recommendations for calculating daily calorie requirements for adults*

Definition: Standard Adult—25-years-old, moderately active and living at a mean environmental temperature of 10 °C.

	Man	Woman
Weight	65 kg	55 kg
Requirement	3 200 kcal	2 300 kcal
Corrections		
Add (or subtract)		
per kg deviation from standard weight	37 kcal	31 kcal
Reduce for increasing age by (%):		
Age (years) 35	3	3
45	6	6
55	14	14
65	21	21
75	31	31
Reduce for each 10 °C		
by which mean annual temperature exceeds 10 °C	5	5
Increase for pregnancy	—	200 kcal
Increase for lactation	—	1 000 kcal

Putting together all these factors to obtain a calculated 'national average' need, gives results of the type shown in Table 7. *A* is a typical developing country with smaller people, a younger age distribution and a warmer climate; *B* is a Western country. There is a difference in the calculated needs 'per head of population', but it is only 20 per cent less for *A* than for *B**.

There is the further question, one that has been considered already in connection with calcium, whether high calorie outputs are really occurring only as a response to high inputs, and whether people could adapt to lower inputs without harm. There have been many claims that religious communities, for example, have evolved a way of life that allowed them to live happily with

* Some national calculations are not expressed on a 'per head' basis, but on 'man units' or 'consumer units' with women and children considered as fractions of a unit with regard to their requirements. It is, of course, essential to be clear about this when attempting to assess the adequacy of a country's food supplies.

TABLE 7. *Calculation of calorie needs per head in two countries 'A' and 'B' according to FAO recommendations*

	A	B
Mean environmental temperature	25 °C	5 °C
Mean adult weight (kg) (men/women)	50/40	70/60
Age distribution (%):		
under 10 years	25	16
10–20	22	13
20–60	47	55
over 60	6	16
Mean need per head per day (kcal)	1 990	2 520

very little food, but where these have been investigated nothing remarkable has been found. In a famous experiment carried out in the University of Minnesota during the Second World War, volunteer students lived for six months on only 1 600 kcal per day. Although they lost a great deal of weight, and were still losing some at the end of the period, they did also show some degree of adaptation, both in basal metabolic rate and in physical activity. To quote from the report, 'they climbed stairs cautiously, one at a time, their responses were sluggish, they were apathetic and showed a curtailment of self-initiated, spontaneous activities'. In other words they were showing one side of the vicious circle, commented on with surprise by visitors to underfed countries, that ordinary people who had a declining standard of living seemed incapable of making the initial effort needed to lift themselves out of the situation. Perhaps they needed the 'get-up-and-go' feeling that would be provided by extra calories; the kind of thing recognized in another species as a horse 'feeling its oats'.

If low calorie intakes were to reduce fertility and thus the birth-rate, this would be a useful self-regulating mechanism for a population outgrowing its food supply. However, there is no evidence of any dramatic effect of chronic under-nutrition on the birth-rate. Even in the famines in parts of Europe during the last war, with all the other disrupting factors, there was generally little effect. In Holland, where the best statistics were kept, it was only at the end of 1944, after a particularly acute period of food shortage, that conceptions dropped sharply. Again, there seems to be surprisingly little effect on the child at birth. Statistics from the same period showed little change in the proportions of stillbirths and malformations, and only about 15 per cent of the children were under their expected birthweight. It is the subsequent growth that suffers from a food shortage.

Resistance to disease is another factor that might be expected to decline with under-nutrition and there has been an historical association between famine and plague. However, other socially disrupting factors may have been more important, since, again in the last War, there were no sweeping epidemics in the concentration camps and the better fed guards had higher death-rates from some diseases than did their prisoners. Only tuberculosis and infantile diarrhoea seemed to be more prevalent amongst the purely malnourished.

The most significant effect of calorie shortage appears therefore to be on physical activity (the straight labour required to produce more food and supplies) and on the power of initiative needed to re-organize things in more efficient ways. The major problem in world food supply is that of producing the extra calories per head to feed the present population adequately, and increasing supplies fast enough to meet the calorie needs of the increasing population. Each mouth needs calories equivalent to 200 kg of grain per year. If at least 400 million more people are to be added to the population of India by the end of the century, they alone will need the equivalent of 80 million tons of grain per year, before standards per head can be raised.

The great bulk of the world's food calories come from the carbohydrates (mostly starch) in the grains and the tubers or roots, such as potatoes or cassava; these give the highest yields of 'digestible calories per hectare' where conditions are suitable for them. Vegetable fat, from oil-seed crops. is also important in some areas. Fats and carbohydrates seem interchangeable sources of calories; there are no standards of requirement for fat as such. On less suitable land, forage plants can be grown and fed to sheep and cattle which are eaten in turn, but this gives a much smaller return of calories per hectare. Possibly some chemical process could be cheapened sufficiently for the direct hydrolysis of cellulose to digestible molecules without the animal (and its intestinal bacteria) having to be used as a convertor. Other unconventional processes have been considered but would have to be very cheap and suitable for operation on a vast scale. What is needed is a carbon chain molecule with some polar group that allows enzymic attack. Petrol molecules have the potential energy but no polar group; conversion to fatty acids was once considered in Germany.

TABLE 8. *Approximate quantities of different classes of foods (expressed as kcalories per head per day) available from net food supply in the United Kingdom and India (1961/62)*

		UK		India	
Cereals		804 ⎫		1 357 ⎫	
Starch foods		187 ⎬ 1 536		28 ⎬ 1 580	
Sugar		545 ⎭		195 ⎭	
Pulses and nuts		52 ⎫ 172		230 ⎫ 257	
Vegetables		120 ⎭		27 ⎭	
Meat		526 ⎫		6 ⎫	
Eggs		61 ⎬ 984		1 ⎬ 114	
Fish		26		3	
Milk		371 ⎭		104 ⎭	
Fats and oils		558		89	
	Total	3 250		2 040	

Fish are likely to remain a valuable supplementary food, rather than to become a staple source of energy. More efficient exploitation of the sea would obviously help but does not introduce any new nutritional principle.

It is difficult for us to reverse our thinking about calories when we move from a local view to a world view. People like ourselves, who can afford to fill our stomachs, find it difficult not to eat more than we need, particularly since our culture is one where human physical work is reduced so much by the availability of machines. A low-calorie food that we can 'fill up on' is a good thing, but it is important to realize what a special case we represent. The contrast between the average person's daily food supply in the United Kingdom and in India is set out in Table 8.

PROTEIN

This is the second class of material needed in large quantities. It forms the machinery of the body, the pumps, muscles, catalysts, membranes and so on. It is needed therefore for growth, but also for maintenance because of the dynamic state of the adult. It is not a single nutrient but a combination of a number. The range of proteins required to build the body tissues is made up of combinations of amino-acids, of which sixteen have been identified as necessary constituents. Proteins are not taken direct from foods by way of the digestive tract to the tissues. They are broken down to amino-acids in the digestive tract and synthesized according to the body's requirements from the amino acids then supplied.

Every protein in the body has an exactly specified structure of amino-acids with perhaps 2000 pieces fitted into each molecule. If one amino-acid is missing, the synthesis stops. Some of the amino-acids can be made in our body from others but there are ten that are essential and can only come from the diet.

It is well known that not all dietary proteins are equally valuable, and that in general, animal protein (i.e. the protein in meat, milk, etc.) is better, i.e. used more efficiently, than vegetable protein from grains, beans etc. The machinery of plants is protein and even grains contain 10 per cent or so, but the proportions of the different amino-acids found in plant tissues are rather different from those used to construct whole animal tissues.

There used to be standards specified for the 'animal protein' content of a diet, but it is now realized that adequate diets can be constructed with very little of these. In most vegetable materials two amino-acids—lysine and methionine—are in short supply, very often at about two-thirds the ideal level. However, this can be compensated for by feeding more of them. Different protein foods are given different 'scores' according to how much is required to provide the most deficient amino-acid in sufficient quantity.

The problems of setting up standards for protein requirement are particularly difficult, with the extra factor of differences in the 'quality' of food proteins having to be taken into account. A critical review of the subject prepared for the Ministry of Health in 1964 by a Committee under the chairmanship of Professor F. G. Young, plotted, for people of different ages, the upper and lower limits of the values suggested as being the requirements, and frankly described the large gap between them as the 'area of ignorance'.

However, two conclusions are generally accepted. First, there is little evidence of physical work increasing protein needs or of there being a practical problem of protein deficiency amongst adults. Secondly, in many of the poorer parts of the world there is a major problem of protein malnutrition amongst children between weaning and four years of age. The local name for the deficiency condition in a part of Ghana is 'kwashiorkor', and this has been adopted internationally as its wider incidence has come to be recognized. It is characterized by oedema (i.e. water-logging of the tissues so that children who are in fact wasted, look unnaturally plump), cracking and scabbiness of the skin and general misery.

Toddlers need a smaller weight of protein per day than adults, but, since they eat so much less, their requirement 'per thousand kcal' is about double that of adults. Wheat, maize and rice which each have about 20 g protein per thousand kcal, can provide most of the child's requirement: only a little supplementary protein is needed. Cassava (tapioca) and bananas have less than 7 g protein per thousand kcal and even children who eat these staples to their full capacity receive only a small fraction of their protein requirements. Generally, other foods richer in protein such as groundnuts, beans and some meat are available at these children's family meals but they may be prepared in highly seasoned curries that the child rejects, or sauces of which a child rarely gets enough. Typically, it is not recognized that the sauces contain food ingredients even more essential for the growing child than for his parents.

In Western countries the traditional and highly successful supplement for the toddler's staple 'energy' foods is cow's milk, but this is not the only supplement possible and it may be too expensive to be generally practicable in the developing countries. Considerable efforts are being made to organize the production of cheaper substitutes. One high-quality material is 'fish flour' prepared from dried de-fatted fish. Vegetable preparations and mixtures have also been prepared, which balance protein-deficient diets. More adventurous programmes involve the separation of the protein from the fibre in grass and leaves, the fermentation of yeasts on by-products and the chemical synthesis of amino-acids.

However, production of protein foods is not always, or even

commonly, the limiting factor. The more difficult problem is for mothers to learn that the children are more demanding in their requirements than the adults, and that they need special foods. Then too, suitable foods in acceptable form must be regularly within the reach of the poorest people.

SUMMING UP

It is always chastening to look back and see how supposedly expert opinions have been wrong in the past. Nevertheless, since there are no alternatives in sight, it does seem that the world will need a continually increasing harvest of more-or-less ordinary staple foods from the fixed total surface of land and water on our planet. These will be needed to provide the calories and most of the protein requirements. Nutrition science and novel developments in food technology may prove useful mainly in providing cheaper 'protective' foods (i.e. rich in protein and vitamins) as alternatives to the traditional milk and meat that are likely to remain out of reach of the poorer peoples, at least in the quantities necessary for them to balance their diets. Whether or not full advantage is taken of these developments will, in turn, depend on the speed of education and the development of a supply organization that is lacking at present.

Fears are sometimes expressed that the nutritive value of foods will be lowered by the means that are proving so successful in giving increased yields—fertilizers, insecticides, herbicides and intensive methods of animal husbandry. Certainly the most intensive checks and research will be needed to guard against this, but we should keep a sense of perspective and remember that the highest death-rates and incidence of crippling disablements, particularly amongst young children, are found where low-yield, natural foods are eaten.

To epitomize the situation, we are foreseeing a 'bread-and-margarine' rather than a 'bread-and-butter' world, and it will take all the skills and efforts of the farmers and industrialists to produce enough even of that type of diet.

CHAPTER 6

AVAILABLE FOOD SUPPLIES

by B. H. Farmer

The purpose of this chapter is, as I see it, to provide a link between the theme of human need in a period of expanding populations expounded in earlier chapters, and that of available resources, physical, biological, technical and social, to be discussed in the chapters which follow. This will involve a discussion of the food supplies at present available, of the current causes of surpluses in some countries and of famines in others, and of trade as a means of moving surpluses to areas of shortage.

My subject may appear, as in some lights it is, a dull and factual one, lacking both the disturbing but stimulating quality of a statement of human need and the rousing practicality of a discussion of available means. I have therefore tabulated the basic facts, or alleged facts, about the situation I am to describe; and propose to comment briefly on the tables rather than to dwell in detail on their factual contents in what might well turn out to be vain and wearisome repetition. It should be noted that a dash in the tables means that no relevant figures are quoted in the source given; while the appearance of a zero means that figures are quoted, but are not significant in terms of the units used.

THE RELIABILITY OF DATA

The figures printed in the tables have such an air of authority and of precision that the uninitiate may well be tempted to draw conclusions from them that would in fact be far too firm: indeed, such conclusions do tend to be drawn by economists and others who ought to know better. It is worth spending a little time at this point in considering the reliability of the available data on the subject-matter of this lecture, for the basis of some of the figures quoted is extremely unsure; and it is unfortunately true that the less developed a country, the less accurate are the statistics about it, whereas, for our purposes at any rate, it is just

TABLE 9. *Regional production of certain foodstuffs*

(in million metric tons)

	Wheat		Barley		Potatoes		Maize		Rice (milled)		Milk		Meat	
	Average 1958–62 (prelim.)	1966 (prelim.)	Average 1958–62 (prelim.)	1966 (prelim.)	Average 1958–62 (prelim.)	1966 (prelim.)	Average 1958–62 (prelim.)	1966 (prelim.)	Average 1958–62 (prelim.)	1966 (prelim.)	Average 1958–62 (prelim.)	1966 (prelim.)	Average 1958–62 (prelim.)	1966 (prelim.)
W. Europe	41·37	44·48	21·74	32·91	74·38	65·10	13·15	18·00	—	—	102·69	112·79	13·75	17·09
E. Europe	13·2	17·4	5·8	7·0	61·8	65·9	10·4	12·5	—	—	28·9	31·2	4·2	5·1
USSR	69·4	100·4	14·4	27·8	82·3	87·2	11·7	8·3	—	—	61·7	75·8	8·7	10·8
N. America	46·07	58·65	13·38	14·86	13·98	16·25	93·68	105·83	1·61	2·51	64·40	62·79	18·03	21·84
Oceania	6·95	12·49	—	—	—	—			—	—	11·80	13·33	2·29	2·57
Latin America	9·57	10·74	—	—	—	—	23·65	31·61	4·81	5·34	19·76	21·57	7·64	8·15
Far East	16·28	16·56	6·36	6·78	—	—	11·64	14·04	88·53	100·99	30·41	34·88	2·97	3·50
Near East	16·70	18·82	2·71	1·60	—	—	3·45	3·95	1·74	2·35	10·94	11·55	1·34	1·56
Africa	3·84	3·03			—	—	12·41	13·60	2·16	2·44	9·08	10·15	2·10	2·40

SOURCE: *The State of Food and Agriculture, 1967* (Rome, FAO, 1967), pp. 156–8.

TABLE 10. *Indices of food production per caput*

(Average 1952–6 = 100)

	1952	1953	1954	1955	1956	1957	1958	1959	1960	1961	1962	1963	1964	1965 (prelim.)
W. Europe	94	101	101	102	102	104	106	108	114	112	118	118	118	118
E. Europe and USSR	93	96	96	103	111	113	122	122	122	124	125	118	128	129
N. America	103	100	97	100	101	96	101	100	100	97	98	104	100	101
Oceania	101	103	98	101	97	92	107	103	107	105	112	113	116	106
Latin America	97	98	100	100	104	103	105	101	100	101	100	102	104	101
Far East (excl. Mainland China)	95	99	100	102	104	102	104	107	109	110	108	109	110	105
Near East	96	103	98	98	105	107	108	109	106	105	110	111	108	107
Africa	97	100	102	99	102	99	100	102	104	100	103	104	104	101

SOURCE: *The State of Food and Agriculture, 1967* (Rome, FAO, 1967), pp. 153–4.

77

the least developed countries that tend to have the most critical food problem. It should also be stressed here that in the absence of reliable and consistent data about Mainland (or Communist) China, no figures for that vast country are included in the tables —so that the statistics for the 'Far East' are apt to be particularly misleading.

→ Production statistics may conveniently be taken first. Tables 9 and 10 purport to show, respectively, absolute production and indices based on absolute production. Clearly in tables such as these, regional totals are derived from country totals, which are in turn derived from district or county totals, and so on down to village or farm level—unless the data are, as is sometimes the case, merely estimated at, say, district level or higher. At the village or farm level a number of factors make first for under-estimation of crop yields and production. For the figures here are often returned or declared by the cultivator himself, or at any rate by a minor official who is himself a villager with a villager's prejudices and vested interests, often subject, too, to pressures from other villagers. If the true yield per acre or per hectare, or the true production are returned, the fear is that the Government will increase taxes, or compulsorily requisition or purchase part of the crop, as in contemporary India, to feed deficit from surplus areas. In other words, the belief is that, as in other walks of life, it does not pay to be seen to be well off. And, again as in other walks of life, some of them not unfamiliar in Western and developed countries, the tendency is to under-declare, often not by a few per cent but by a very wide margin indeed. A further source of underdeclaration in a number of countries arises from the existence, in times of scarcity and control, of a vigorous black market, from which villagers, or those subject to village pressures, hope to profit.

→ A notorious case of underdeclaration, but one that still misleads the unwary, is provided by statistics for paddy yields in Ceylon. If one looks at the *Statistical Abstract* for that country for the years 1944/5 to 1950/1, one finds that the yield of paddy for the *Maha* season, the main cultivation season, varies from 14·0 to 15·4 Ceylon bushels per acre. But the *Abstract* for 1951/2 gives a yield of 30·9 bushels per acre. Subsequent annual volumes and other sources show a slightly fluctuating, but general improvement on that figure, up to 38·02 bushels per acre in 1961/2 and over 40 bushels per acre in 1967*. Clearly, on *a priori* grounds alone, it is unlikely that Ceylon's paddy fields witnessed an overnight economic miracle, leading to more than a doubling of yields between 1950/1 and 1951/2 (though that has not prevented economists and others, to my certain knowledge, from naïvely taking the figures at their face value). The fact is that the earlier figures were based on returns from the compulsory Internal Purchase Scheme and, later, from village headmen, both sources subject to already-mentioned pressures making for underdeclaration, whereas, from 1951/2 onwards, the figures are the product of random sampling and of crop-cutting experiments. There are some, it should perhaps be said, who feel that the officials concerned in this sampling are under some pressure to please by inflating their returns. But it cannot be gainsaid that random sampling involving crop-cutting experiments is preferable to estimation by local petty officials: though that is not to say that the result has necessarily complete objectivity and an impeccable order of accuracy.

Statistics for yields per acre also suffer from faulty estimation of area cultivated; in the Ceylon case it is thought that area asweddumized, i.e. laid out for paddy cultivation, was, at the time of the institution of sample surveys, overestimated by amounts varying, district by district, from 9–69 per cent. Clearly the effect of such overestimation is to depress yield figures, where these are obtained by dividing production by area.

A second reason for under-enumeration of production lies in a failure, for whatever reason, to record certain categories of cultivated land. In the United Kingdom, for instance, no one ever knew until a very recent enquiry instituted by the Thorpe Committee what was grown on allotment-gardens. (I speak as an allotment-cultivator!) And still no one knows what is produced in ordinary kitchen gardens. In underdeveloped countries, it is even less possible for Government agencies to know the acreage and production of, say, plots subject to shifting cultivation, often lying deep in the jungle, and sometimes growing illicitly such crops as Indian hemp. Some such plots are supposed to be licensed, as in the case of the Ceylon *chenas*, but widespread

* The Ceylon bushel of rice is given as 50 lb: *The Economist Guide to Weights and Measures*, p. 51. In fact it varies over the country.

evasion of the regulations tends to falsify, in the direction of under-enumeration, whatever figures there may be. E. R. Leach writes of the area round Pul Eliya, in the Anuradhapura District of Ceylon:

Judging by my experience of 1954 I should guess that not more than half of the *chenas* in actual use had received any sort of licence from the government. It is also very obvious that only a very small number of these clearings are of the regulation one-acre size; most of them appear to be between four and fifteen acres in extent.

And if this is true of a small country like Ceylon, with a relatively close network of communications and administration, what figures can there be for shifting cultivators' plots in, say, the interior of the Congo or Brazil?

Quite apart from what is grown on unrecorded plots, whole categories of foodstuffs tend to go unrecorded or even to defy enumeration: for instance, those that may be gathered in many countries by foraging in the bush, or from half-wild gardens and trees.

It must not be supposed, however, even with the glaring example of Ceylon paddy statistics in mind, that errors in food production statistics are always in the direction of underestimation, though that is probably by far the commonest form of error. Certain factors may make for considerable overestimation of yields or of the production available for human consumption. For instance:

(1) As has already been hinted, where the pressure is for increased yields, officials may overestimate, or even falsify in the direction of overestimation, in order to win commendation. Villagers, too, have been known to borrow rice plants from neighbouring settlements in order to improve the look of their fields when estimates of yields are being made, especially when prizes are at stake. There may thus be a tendency, when pressures for increased yields are suddenly appreciated, for yield figures equally suddenly to cross a threshold from underestimation to overestimation.

(2) If crop-sampling or estimation from the standing crop is attempted before it is ripe, or if the harvest is for any reason delayed, the crop may lodge or grain may shed and up to one-third may be lost—or more if a severe storm supervenes. This source of overestimation was one of the many subjects on which Mr Khruschev pronounced when in office.

↝ (3) Even if harvest yields or production figures are correct
they may be a most inaccurate guide to what is available for consumption because of loss between field and consumer caused by
birds, rats, fungi, insects, children and other pests; or by
leakages in transit because of holes, literal or metaphorical, in
sacks, lorries or railway wagons. Metaphorical holes do not, of
course, subtract from the total amount available for consumption, though they may divert foodstuffs into hoards or other
socially undesirable repositories, and involve delayed consumption. Some think that as much as one-third of the grain
harvested in India is lost to consumption for one reason or
another; others have suggested that the proportion is as high as
one-half; recent reports from Delhi suggest an over-all loss of
5–10 per cent, of which rodents account for 2·4 per cent. The
truth is that no one knows the rate of loss: there may even be
vested interests that overestimate it!

⟋ (4) It is also, of course, necessary to subtract from crude
yields and production figures of grain production the amounts
fed to stock or used as seed.

Finally, there are a number of sources of error that are more
nearly random in their effect, or that, at all events, sometimes
depress, sometimes exaggerate yield or production figures. For
example:

(1) There may be official falsification of figures for one reason
or another: for instance, when a 'surplus' area wishes to conceal the size of its supplies to avoid procurement of them in
favour of 'deficit' areas. Such falsification is more easily sus-
pected than proved, and when known cannot always be published.

(2) It is often difficult to make more than a wild guess at the
production of such sources of starch, widely grown in the
Tropics, as yams and manioc (cassava, *Manihot utilissima*). In
the absence of farm or plot data, one can count sacks of grain
passing a check-point, but it is much more difficult to assess by
similar means a lorry-load, or part load, of tubers in the loose.

(3) It is not unknown for errors, one way or the other, to arise
from the use of faulty conversion factors. Thus the earlier
editions of Pierre Gourou's *The Tropical World* contained a
faulty conversion from bushels per acre to kilograms per hectare
(*cf.* Gourou, 1963, p. 16 and 1961, p. 16); and a bushel of grain

does not everywhere contain the same weight of grain (even within Ceylon, as has been seen).

(4) Figures for production or consumption per head of the population are often cited and, of course, constitute a most useful index when they can be trusted: but, even if production and consumption figures are reliable, the population figures by which these must be divided to arrive at an answer *per caput* may often be seriously in error. Under-enumeration in censuses is more common than over-enumeration; and errors in the same direction arise from under-registration of births when population figures have to be derived from such sources as Registrar-Generals' inter-censal estimates. But overestimates of population for political reasons are sometimes alleged. Again, the more underdeveloped the country, the less reliable are both census and registration data.

(5) Finally, even where every effort is made to secure objectivity, for example by correctly designed random sampling, there necessarily remain errors of a statistical nature of a sort that will be perfectly familiar to anyone with a knowledge of elementary statistics. In this connection, the *Statistical Abstract for Ceylon* has, since it began to quote crop yields based on random sampling, also included figures for the standard error involved.

Clearly, then, there is great need for caution in accepting figures for yield and production of foodstuffs, whether in absolute terms or relative to population. Yet cases are not unknown of governments being misled by their own statistics. Colin Clark and M. R. Haswell suggest that the Government of India in the early 1950's thought the shortage of grain dangerous, and were willing to devote scarce foreign exchange to its alleviation, because they were misled by production figures subject to grave underdeclaration during a period of compulsory purchase and black marketing.

Estimates of calorie intake, such as those set out, for what they are worth, in Table 11, are by and large even less reliable, and, once again, the less developed the country, the less reliable its data. The reasons for this state of affairs will by now be fairly obvious, and need only be stated briefly. One approach to figures for daily *per caput* consumption of calories is through figures for production and population; this carries the

TABLE 11. *Tentative estimated calorie content of national average food supplies*

	Calories/day (year as shown)		Calories/day (year as shown)
EUROPE		S. Africa	2820 (1960–1)
Austria	2970 (1965–6)	Tanganyika	2110 (1961–3)
Belgium	3080 (1964–5)	Uganda	2310 (1961)
Denmark	3310 (1965–6)		
Finland	2950 (1964–5)	NEAR EAST	
France	2970 (1964–5)	Afghanistan	2050 (1962)
Germany, Fed. Rep.	2910 (1965–6)	Iran	2050 (1960)
Greece	2960 (1963)	Iraq	2100 (1960–2)
Hungary	3020 (1965)	Israel	2820 (1964–5)
Ireland	3460 (1964)	Jordan	2390 (1964)
Italy	2780 (1965–6)	Lebanon	2730 (1965)
Jugoslavia	3110 (1963)	Libya	1910 (1964)
Netherlands	2920 (1965–6)	Sudan	1950 (1964)
Norway	2970 (1965–6)	Syria	2360 (1963)
Poland	3350 (1960–2)	Turkey	3110 (1960–1)
Portugal	2640 (1965)	United Arab Republic	2930 (1963–4)
Romania	3020 (1963)		
Spain	2850 (1963–4)	OCEANIA	
Sweden	3000 (1965–6)	Australia	3160 (1964–5)
Switzerland	3160 (1964–5)	New Zealand	3460 (1965)
United Kingdom	3250 (1965–6)		
		LATIN AMERICA	
N. AMERICA		Argentina	3100 (1964)
Canada	3130 (1965–6)	Bolivia	1860 (1963)
United States	3140 (1965)	Brazil	2950 (1964)
		Chile	2560 (1963)
FAR EAST		Colombia	2250 (1964)
Ceylon	2080 (1965)	Costa Rica	2460 (1963)
China (Taiwan)	2380 (1965)	Dominican Rep.	2230 (1964)
India	2110 (1964–5)	Ecuador	1830 (1963)
Indonesia	1980 (1961–3)	El Salvador	2120 (1962)
Japan	2350 (1965)	Guatemala	2320 (1962)
Pakistan	2260 (1964–5)	Honduras	2070 (1962)
Philippines	2070 (1965)	Jamaica	2240 (1958)
		Mexico	2640 (1962)
AFRICA		Nicaragua	2550 (1962)
Ethiopia	2040 (1961–3)	Panama	2480 (1964)
Ghana	2030 (1961–3)	Paraguay	2730 (1963)
Kenya	2120 (1961–3)	Peru	2150 (1963)
Madagascar	2220 (1962)	Surinam	2120 (1964)
Mauritius	2310 (1965)	Uruguay	3220 (1960–2)
Somalia	1780 (1961–3)	Venezuela	2240 (1963)

SOURCE: FAO, *Production Yearbook,* vol. 20, 1966 (Rome, FAO, 1967), p. 422–6.

consequences of any unreliability in these data, exaggerated, however, by the virtual impossibility of ascertaining with any accuracy the nature and amount of loss between producer and consumer. There is also the problem of loss in milling or other processes, which may vary, in the case of wheat, from zero in the wholemeal beloved by the food faddists to, perhaps, 10 per cent in poor countries and to 33 per cent in the case of white bread in 'advanced' countries; or, in the case of rice, from a minimum of 20 per cent to 40 per cent, depending, it would appear, more on dietetic prejudice and preference than on the need to conserve grain content through poverty.

Another approach is that through the study of consumption and, in particular, of sample diets. The data collected for, say, a single Pakistani family may then be of fair accuracy; but there are severe problems in designing the sample to be surveyed, especially in a country with wide differences between one region and another and between classes or castes within a region. Brahmins and banias (moneylenders) in India may, for example, consume twice as many calories in a day as a landless labourer or cultivator, and look like it. One meets, in fact, many strata in one's sample. Similar considerations apply, with even greater force, to estimates of the protein and vitamin content of average national diets.

It must be said, in all fairness, that these and other limitations are firmly underlined by FAO in presenting, in the annual *Production Yearbook*, tables of the calorie, fat and protein content of national diets, based on national 'food balance sheets'; and, equally, in presenting the results of certain national food consumption surveys, whose results by no means tally with those derived from balance sheets. In 1954, figures for calorie content of diets were given for thirty-nine countries, and compared with pre-war figures. But in 1955, data were presented on a new basis for twenty countries only. Since that date the number of countries for which figures have been published has increased annually save only in 1960 and 1961. The latest available table covers seventy-one countries; it is reproduced in Table 11. It is a little hard to see how Clark and Haswell can claim that '... countries for which information is now published constitute a much shorter list than that which was published a few years ago'; though, of course, one cannot be sure that newcomers to the list are at all accurately or contemporarily represented by their statistics, while others are represented by time series containing marked breaks.

TABLE 12. *Grain stocks*

(in million metric tons)

	1961	1962	1963	1964	1965	1966	1967 forecast
WHEAT							
USA	38·4	36·0	32·5	24·5	22·3	14·6	11·2
Canada	16·5	10·6	13·3	12·5	14·0	11·4	16·0
Argentina	0·8	0·2	0·5	2·2	3·3	0·2	0·1
Australia	0·7	0·5	0·6	0·6	0·7	0·5	2·0
France	1·9	1·7	3·2	2·3	2·0	2·6	1·9
Total, five major exporters	58·3	49·0	50·1	42·1	42·3	29·3	31·2
COARSE GRAINS							
USA	77·2	65·4	58·2	62·9	50·1	38·6	29·5
Canada	4·5	2·8	4·5	5·7	4·2	4·5	5·7
Total, two major exporters	81·7	68·2	62·7	68·6	54·3	43·1	35·2

SOURCE: *The State of Food and Agriculture, 1967*
(Rome, FAO, 1967), p. 164.

Figures for Grain Stocks (Table 12) are probably trustworthy for the countries cited, but, were underdeveloped countries included, data for these might well be subject to very considerable error.

Trade Statistics (Table 13) are for the most part much more reliable, based as they are on such sources as customs returns. (It will be noted that Table 13 refers to different years from those covered by earlier tables.) They do, however, pose a number of problems: for example, the item 'Exports' usually includes re-exports (which explains why Belgium, in the source from which the table derives, appears as an exporter of rice). It should also be noted that the regional total in the table is the sum of the relevant national totals, so that the trade of a region, like Western Europe, that comprises many small countries is exaggerated, compared with a region like North America containing a few large countries. In fact, the table does not represent inter-regional trade.

TABLE 13. *Trade in selected foodstuffs*
(in thousand metric tons)

	Wheat		Barley		Maize		Rice		Potatoes		Meat		Butter and cheese	
	1963	1964	1963	1964	1963	1964	1963	1964	1963	1964	1963	1964	1963	1964
EXPORTS														
W. Europe	3481	3762	2293	3147	836	1255	235	188	1646	1698	850	792	625	625
E. Europe	467	23	92	112	1113	340	11	50	460	1150	256	246	49	54
USSR	4106	2030	594	666	723	839	12	4	—	—	145	52	69	30
N. America	28282	34766	1618	2475	11177	12521	1202	1333	320	282	323	373	57	95
Latin America	1879	3710	45	539	3154	3411	177	145	19	19	753	702	21	17
Near East	195	218	538	293	2	2	18	24	126	135	0	1	2	2
Far East (excl. Mainland China)	12	11	—	—	919	1340	4084	4210	36	49	12	42	0	0
Africa	133	117	169	108	2931	1625	419	567	253	221	47	52	6	5
Oceania	4136	6905	234	403	10	0	58	57	20	17	884	928	366	394
IMPORTS														
W. Europe	9928	9385	3558	4450	13840	14369	529	548	1708	1543	1988	2152	927	993
E. Europe	6181	6437	959	1227	1005	1323	344	300	349	1041	305	159	114	72
USSR	3052	7281	—	—	—	—	194	363	—	—	27	89	5	8
N. America	651	634	224	348	1244	964	358	457	180	239	631	455	67	68
Latin America	3191	4023	48	55	10	252	9	74	99	116	22	33	25	25
Near East	1641	834	259	104	286	279	394	343	68	91	23	29	19	22
Far East (excl. Mainland China)	10420	12050	389	678	3103	3546	4207	3348	139	152	131	182	25	36
Africa	2151	1860	26	50	346	655	565	695	334	347	54	59	60	63
Oceania	181	178	—	—	1	1	44	47	8	8	7	10	5	5

Source: FAO Trade Yearbook, 1964.

THE PRODUCTION OF FOODSTUFFS

Table 9, based on figures published by FAO, is an attempt to show the regional production of a number of basic foodstuffs and gives averages for the years 1958–62 together with preliminary figures for the year 1966. I do not propose to comment on the figures in detail, for this would defeat the object of publishing the table. In spite of the reservations on the reliability of data that are so necessary when studying tables of this sort, it is nevertheless possible to draw a number of conclusions from it. For instance:

(1) The orders of magnitude involved can be discerned—e.g. annual world production of wheat during the years 1958–62 was about 200 million metric tons, and of milled rice about 100 million metric tons, neglecting production in Mainland China.

(2) The broad regional distribution of production is clear: thus about one-third of the world's wheat is produced in the USSR, about one-fifth in each of Western Europe and North America, and so on; while something of the order of 90 per cent of the world's rice production is concentrated in the Far East, which here includes India, Pakistan and Ceylon but not, of course, Mainland China, inclusion of whose figures could not but increase the preponderance of the region. Again, the relatively paltry output of milk and meat outside the more advanced regions is all too clear, and an important cause of protein shortage, if not protein deficiency, stands revealed. India has, of course an enormous national herd of cows, most of them with a pathetic yield—to be measured in pints rather than gallons per day during lactation. It should also be pointed out that the source used for the table, together with the annual FAO *Production Yearbook*, gives production details by countries, and also for foodstuffs other than those included in Table 9.

Trends in Production are hinted at in Table 9, but emerge more clearly from Table 10, subject always, of course, to a *caveat* about the accuracy of data—a *caveat* that cannot be too often reiterated. It will be noticed that the index chosen by FAO is based on food production for the years 1952–6. Average annual food production in each region for that period and for other years shown is measured in terms of a long standard list of commodities, ranging from grains and starchy roots to fruits,

cocoa and the welcome products of the vine, deducting only production flowing back into the agricultural sector, for example, as
animal feeding-stuffs: this means, *inter alia*, that plant-derived
starch used in industry is counted as agricultural production
even though one dines in, but not on starched shirts. The
indices for all years are, further, weighted according to a formula
that need not be explained here.

The indices, for all the long shadows cast over them by the
gaunt inadequacies of the data behind them, are at least on a
per caput basis, so that they give some indication of the extent to
which food production is keeping pace with growing population.
Once again, the table will repay detailed and thoughtful study,
and little need be said by way of comment. It may perhaps be
stressed, however, that, if the indices are to be trusted, Western
Europe, Eastern Europe and the USSR have increased their
food production *per caput* by 20 per cent or so over the average
for the base years, though with some fluctuations, and Oceania,
(that is, essentially, Australia and New Zealand) by rather less.
The fourth 'advanced' region, North America, has however,
barely changed its production of food *per caput*, a fact that should
be borne in mind when one listens to airy talk about the vast food
surpluses of Canada and the United States. The four less-
developed regions, and it must be remembered once again that
the indices take no account of production in Mainland China,
appear to be like North America at least in this respect, for they
show food production as gaining only slightly and hesitantly on
population increase; in some years the index slips back as in
1965, while in most regions, except in the Near East, all that has
been done since the war is to regain pre-war levels of food production in relation to population.

The superficial similarity in the run of the indices for North
America and for the far less-developed regions conceals a
fundamental contrast. In North America, food production has
long been at a level that provides an ample diet for the whole
population, together with a surplus rather larger than could be
conveniently disposed of by normal international trade. Hence
American policy has been concerned on the one hand with con-
cessionary disposal to such deficit countries as India, and on the
other with a deliberate policy of restricting the growth of
agricultural production. In the less developed regions, on the

other hand, all the effort devoted to agricultural productivity has achieved little more than the maintenance of *per caput* production.

It should also be noted that, if one were to look at world indices, one would discover that food production in the world as a whole is barely keeping pace with population increase. Moreover, it is clear that in 1965 world food production suffered a setback: for in almost all other regions, by and large, the year was one of droughts and poor harvests. Indeed, underdeveloped countries increased their food imports by 4 per cent. There was some recovery in production in 1966 and 1967.

One footnote may usefully be added. The unwary may draw the conclusion from the static, near-static or even declining indices for some of the regions that there has been no improvement in agriculture during the period covered by Table 10. This would, in many countries, be a false conclusion. In India, for example, absolute data suggest that food-grain production increased by over 25 per cent between 1949–50 and 1961–2: that is, at a compound rate of 3·45 per cent *per annum*. Improving yields accounted, it seems, for 1·75 per cent *per annum*, the extension of cultivation on to newly won, or at any rate newly-recorded, land presumably accounting for the rest. But during the same period the compound population growth rate was 2·0 per cent *per annum*—greater, at any rate, than the rate of increase in yield, giving one pause to think what will be the result of the exhaustion, probably in the not very distant future of land available for the extension of cultivation at existing technical levels and without prohibitive cost. These figures highlight the basic problem in countries like India: the problem is not so much that production has not increased, but that it has not increased fast enough in relation to population growth, and that it is not easy to see how even the rates of increase of production achieved so far can be maintained. Moreover, it is also true in India (and, no doubt, elsewhere) that people have rising expectations, that whereas famine in the nineteenth century meant no food, it now means less than one, or perhaps two square meals a day: so that famine is a political problem too. I am greatly indebted to Dr Daniel Thorner for a discussion of this problem; though I must emphasize that the words used are my own. But whatever the truth on this score, and whatever the view one takes of the statistics, there can be no doubt that, as one contemplates present rates of population growth and, even more, future projections, the clouds gather and the scene darkens.

THE QUESTION OF CALORIE INTAKE AND ITS ADEQUACY

Time and space forbid discussion of components of diet other than calories, and, in any case, data for proteins and vitamins are particularly shaky, as has already been said. But a word must be said about what appears to be the intake of calories in various countries in relation to dietetic need. The leading role of calorie intake in the whole nutritional process and in the provision of energy to be used, *inter alia*, in work was set out in Chapter 5 and the arguments about the needs of populations of differing age structure in differing climatic environments and confronted with differing amounts of work to be done have been discussed. Clearly the number of calories *per caput* required by a given population, even if its main parameters are known, is still a matter of debate. Clark and Haswell produce a calculation to show that the populations in India and South-east Asia need daily 1625 calories *per caput* if the men work a four-hour day; but 1821 calories if they work an eight-hour day. P. K. Sukhatme on the other hand, arrives after an elaborate calculation at 2100 calories *per caput* as the daily need of the Indian population, or 2250–2300 calories at the retail level to allow for subsequent wastage.

For reasons that should by now have been made abundantly clear, the figures for average daily *per caput* calorie intake summarized in Table 11 must be accepted with great reserve. Suppose, however, that one takes 2300 calories as the Indian requirement at the retail level, matches this against the 2110 calories shown in the table, and hence arrives at a daily deficit *per caput* of about 200 calories. Accepting the figures at their face value, and assuming for the purposes of the exercise that the whole of the deficit is to be met by supplying wheat subject to 10 per cent loss in milling, the annual Indian need is then for something, very roughly, of the order of an additional 13 million metric tons, and this in a reasonably good year. Clearly, if Sukhatme's assumption on calorie requirements under Indian conditions is correct, and if Table 11 correctly states the present intake, then, nothing short of a massive improvement in Indian food supplies, and in particular grain supplies, is called for; and this most observers of the Indian scene would believe to be true. On the other hand, if one assumes with Clark and Haswell that the *per caput* requirement of calories is a great deal lower, then Indian needs in calories are already met by supplies: this on all sorts of grounds, is hard to believe. At the very least, it is a matter of common, qualitative observation that very substantial sectors of Indian society are badly undernourished in terms of calories—to say nothing of shortages of proteins and vitamins. And what is true of India is also no doubt true of many other countries, as those with personal knowledge and experience can testify.

Given uncertainty not only about the absolute size of food supplies but also about basic nutritional needs, it is clearly not possible to say with confidence that, say, 42·7 per cent of mankind are under-nourished, or even that one-half, or one-third of our fellows are in that sad condition. What cannot be gainsaid, even by Clark and Haswell, is that malnutrition afflicts very large numbers of people in the world as a whole, and high proportions of the population in underdeveloped countries, in which levels of food consumption are well below those in advanced countries; and further, that the effect of population increase is bound, in the absence of drastic changes in the supply of foodstuffs, to lead to increasing strain in the future, particularly in countries like India where the supply of suitable new land waiting to be broken for cultivation is severely limited if not already virtually non-existent. N. C. Wright's statement in 1961 that each additional 100 million people need some 13 million tons of cereals to give them an adequate diet is perhaps an exaggeration because of the high daily calorie intake he postulated (2800 calories *per caput* daily); but it is instructive to match some such figure against the quantities in Tables 9 and 10.

FAMINE

What also cannot be gainsaid, in spite of the remarks already made about the effect of 'rising expectations', is the very real fact of recurrent famine in some parts of at least some countries. This state of famine, or at least of severe shortage, is sometimes a seasonal matter, recurring almost every year, as in parts of the African savanna. Elsewhere, as in India until comparatively recent times, famines have been an irregularly recurring phenomenon, but one that was disastrous when it struck.

The proximate cause of irregularly recurring famine is, of course, usually the failure of the harvest for natural causes, such as drought. There are many countries in which, as in India, agriculture is a perpetual gamble with the rains. Sometimes the proximate cause lies elsewhere, as in the Bengal famine of 1943 (which I witnessed, and shall not easily forget), where what was mainly at issue was the failure of customary sources of food imports under wartime conditions, combined with hoarding and racketeering.

But deeper causes lie behind most famines, including seasonal ones. For if the cultivator, together with the agricultural labourer and other members of the rural community, were able to produce enough to save stocks, or to save money with which to purchase foodstuffs in lean years, all but the worst famines might be averted. In countries like India famine is nowadays also a matter of the urban population, which is likewise beaten in times of food shortage by a lack of stocks or of money savings in the face of rising prices; these, of course, also rise more than would otherwise be the case because of hoarding and other anti-social practices, not always helped by government action.

Behind these phenomena again lie a whole complex of economic, social and political conditions, not all of them understood and not all beyond the range of controversy, which bear, in one way or another, on rural productivity in relation to population growth. Some of the non-controversial or less controversial components in this complex may be taken to include:

(1) Population increase associated with a declining area of cultivated land *per caput* and, hence, other things remaining the same, a declining food production *per caput*.

(2) A further consequence of population increase, namely, the extension of cultivation on to less and less productive land, yielding decreasing returns.

(3) The monetization of the economy, often under the impact of Western commerce, leading, *inter alia*, to the sort of hoarding and withholding of supplies that played such a disastrous part in the Bengal famine of 1943.

(4) The setting of the terms of trade against the cultivator, or at least against agricultural labour, so that static income is confronted by rising prices for goods consumed and, possibly, by rising rents.

(5) A general failure of technology to respond sufficiently quickly, or in the right direction, in the face of population increase: for example, a failure to make the transition from shifting cultivation to a sedentary agriculture yielding higher and more stable yields per acre, or a failure to respond to the provision of irrigation water. It is the thesis of Ester Boserup in her book *The Conditions of Agricultural Growth* (1965) that population growth is the main agency by means of which agrarian progress is brought about; but she admits that a society does not necessarily respond to population growth by accepting or developing improved agricultural practices.

Elements in the social, economic and political environment that, although accepted by some authorities to have this or that effect on productivity, are nonetheless the subjects of controversy, include:

(1) The manipulation by governments, for economic or social or political reasons, or for some mixture of motives, more usually of conditions of land tenure: for example, by instituting collective of cooperative cultivation, or by 'land reforms' by means of which it is intended to put title to land in the hands of the tiller rather than the landlord, or by imposing conditions on the cultivation or alienation of land, as in the Ceylon peasant colonization schemes.

(2) Another controversial subject is that of the agrarian effects of imperialism, or, at any rate, of the experience of imperialism. There are some who hold with that serious though armchair student of India, Karl Marx, that under British imperial rule such linked phenomena, or alleged linked phenomena, as high land revenue rates, indebtedness, the concentration of land in a few hands, the driving of unemployed rural craftsmen, whose products could not compete with imported goods, into agricultural labour, and the export of foodgrains all contributed very significantly to the present distressing state of Indian agriculture and, in particular, to its relatively low productivity. Doubt may, however, be cast on some parts at least of this thesis: for instance, Dr Dharma Kumar has recently demon-

strated that a large agricultural labour force, some of it in slavery, and mainly based on caste, antedates British rule in South India. Time and space prevent any further exploration of the complex forces that lie behind a failure of agricultural production to keep pace with population growth and hence a continuing potential instability which all too readily erupts into famine with the failure of the rains or the cessation of customary imports.

Surpluses need not long detain us, partly because agricultural production on a perennially assured basis is more familiar to us in the West; partly because surpluses arise, in general, from the opposites of many of the adverse conditions just outlined. Thus, in general, it has been the existence in the West of a more developed, and indeed a rapidly developing, technology which, under generally favourable natural conditions, has brought about the rising productivity per man employed and per acre cultivated that has revolutionized agriculture in such countries as Britain and the United States, and that, amongst other things, built up from about 1952 the huge stocks of grains that totalled 140 million tonnes in 1961 (see Table 12). Latterly, of course, the United States in particular has taken measures to restrain production. It will be noticed, however, that the total wheat stock in 1961 was only some 56 million tonnes, enough, on Sukhatme's assumptions and given the calculation already made, for about four years' supply of the balance necessary to bring Indian calorie intake up to that which is necessary. Since 1961 wheat stocks in the four principal exporting countries have halved, moreover; and there was a steep decline (18 per cent) in American PL. 480 exports in 1965. Or, to put the matter another way, even if the assured American surplus were to continue at a level of 10 million tonnes annually, it would provide enough only for about a half of the annual Indian shortfall, on the same assumptions. And, of course, the problems of shipping, handling and organizing the transport of so much grain for such a long haul would be insuperable. Moreover, quite apart from government action, the surplus in the main exporting countries is also liable to erosion by the growth of their own populations, except so far as productivity continues to increase.

TRADE

The state of world trade in foodstuffs in 1963 and 1964 is summarized in Table 13. As with other tables, the figures are meant to speak for themselves, and no detailed commentary will be attempted. The table does, however, identify the chief exporters and importers of wheat, rice and other important foodstuffs. It must also be said that the greatest increase in post-war international trade in food has been between advanced countries, notably between European countries; but that there is rather more than a hint of a tendency for most underdeveloped regions to import more foodstuffs, particularly wheat, in order to maintain their food supplies—at a time when the terms of trade are generally set against them, thus accentuating balance of payment problems. Moreover, many pre-war food exporters have ceased to export; and very recently indeed Ceylon, an habitual importer of rice, has found great difficulty in securing adequate supplies from traditional sources like Burma and Thailand. The import of wheat by underdeveloped countries of course involves changing food habits for some of them, especially the rice-eaters.

CONCLUSION

My theme, in retrospect, is, then, a simple one. Although many basic statistics are of very doubtful accuracy and although there is by no means universal agreement on dietary needs, it cannot be denied that there is a serious food problem in many countries—seasonal, or periodic, or perpetual; and that, given current rates of population growth, there is a compelling need for remedial action. But the distribution of other countries' surpluses, through trade or through aid, is an insufficient answer, and appears to be growing less and less of an answer. The only possible solution apart from population control is improvement in agricultural production and productivity in the underdeveloped countries, which need all the technical and other assistance it is possible to give them.

CHAPTER 7

LAND TENURE AND PRODUCTIVITY

by William Allan

Land tenure implies the assertion of individual or group rights over land. It is one of the most ancient of human institutions. Increasing populations and the vast land areas required to support hunting and food-gathering economies must have given rise to concepts of exclusive rights at a very early stage of the human story. Forms of 'land tenure' are found in many recent and surviving cultures with such economies. It appears to have been true of most hunting and collecting peoples that each group within the tribal community possessed rights of exploitation over an extensive area defined by natural boundaries. This was the hunting and food-gathering 'territory'. The group or 'band' associated with each territory was usually a shallow lineage—a very few closely related families. They inherited their rights and held them exclusively. A group might permit outsiders to use their land but trespass was forbidden on pain of sorcery or death. Quite commonly, a senior member of the group, the titular 'owner', exercised a sort of wardenship over the natural resources of the territory but his 'ownership' was expressed only in supervising and safeguarding the inalienable rights of other members.

Patterns of this general type, with variations which are clearly related to environmental ecology and regional resources, have been described for many North and South American tribes, Australian Aborigines, Bushmen and other hunting and food-gathering peoples. Among the living Bushmen of the Kalahari the pattern remains intact. Each group has a very specific territory which that group alone may use, and its boundaries are rigidly respected.

With the advent of agriculture, the primary exploiting unit changed from the band to the single cultivating family. The rights of the cultivating family became entrenched in the area of actual cultivation but tribal and group rights over land in general persisted. This type of situation is commonly referred to as communal tenure. It is communal in the sense that communities, or those who act in trust for them, exercise rights of administration and control, but there is a firm underlying stratum of individual rights in cultivated land. Communal ownership and exploitation of wild products, fishing waters and pasturage is much more clearly marked.

The emergence of civilizations with large political units, and the concomitant social and economic problems, brought all sorts of innovations and experiments in agrarian organization; in the relationship between the individual, the land and the community. From this emerged concepts of private ownership of land, divorced from actual exploitation, and tenure by tenancy. Many scholars see in Solon's reforms of the sixth century B.C. the beginning of the institution of private property in land in Ancient Greece. Previously, land was held and worked by individuals but the title vested in the clan or family. It was inalienable to outsiders and transfers of land were permissible only within the clan or family, primarily by inheritance. A similar system of communal clan tenure persisted in the highlands of Scotland until the 'pacification' following the Jacobite rebellion of 1745.

All of these forms of tenure operate in the world today, sometimes side by side, and we have also the new institutions of the countries with centrally planned and directed economies. The varying relationships between men and land which this situation implies have a strong bearing on the productivity of agriculture and the problems of development. The way in which these problems and their solutions are perceived also varies greatly from country to country. For purposes of brief review, we will consider the situation within a framework of four groups of countries at different levels of economic development and with varying forms of land tenure: (1) developing countries with communal forms of tenure; (2) developing countries with private ownership of land; (3) economically advanced countries with private ownership of land, and (4) countries with centrally-planned economies.

COMMUNAL TENURES

Communal tenures remain the dominant form of land holding throughout inter-tropical Africa and in some territories of the Pacific. Elsewhere, as in many South American countries, China (Taiwan) and some Indian States, these forms exist side by side with private property rights, but they usually affect only a minority of the population, the 'indigenous' or 'tribal' peoples. Most of the following discussion relates more specifically to Africa, which is by far the most important area in which communal tenure is still dominant.

One feature common to all of these forms is that they are based on customary observance. They suffer from the imprecision inevitable in any system of unwritten rights. The question of rights over fallow is particularly important to the permanence of the food-producing systems. In general, traditional systems of agriculture depend for the maintenance of fertility on a period of fallow in one form or another. Other forms of fertility maintenance are also employed, but the fallow is normally an essential element. The duration of this break is enormously variable. It may be as much as twenty years or it may be one year or less. This is determined by the environment and the character of the soil, its durability under cultivation and the rapidity with which fertility is restored under the conditions of the fallow. In inter-tropical Africa there are vast areas of ferrallitic, ferruginous tropical and weakly developed soils of poor durability and very low regenerative capacity. For this reason, systems with long or very long fallow periods are prevalent. But there are also limited areas of eutrophic and other soils of high agricultural value and rapid regenerative power. On such soils, very short fallow periods and virtually permanent cultivation systems are the rule.

In the case of a long-fallow system, we may think of the production unit, the 'farm', as a relatively large area only a fraction of which—commonly one-quarter to one-eighth—is in cultivation at any one time. The remainder is in different stages of regeneration, and the cultivated area is rotated over the whole in such a way as to preserve the fallow-cultivation balance and maintain the fertility of the soil. These two parts are, in effect, held under different forms of tenure. In the cultivated part, rights vested in the individual are dominant, but over the fallow, community rights are stronger. Quite commonly, resting land is 'identified' with the village or lineage rather than with the individual who previously cultivated it. This may be of little practical significance while there is sufficient land, but when a stage of over-population is reached—in the sense of an excess of population over what I have called the Critical Density—or when cash cropping or, in some cases, the introduction of the plough, has produced similar effects, encroachment on the fallow is inevitable. The cultivator's claim to his fallow is superseded by the greater right of the community. Where men can live only by cultivation, the land must be shared whatever the consequences.

With reduction of the fallow, fertility declines, sometimes imperceptibly at first, but the process is a vicious spiral. As yields fall more land must be cultivated, the fallow is further reduced and the rate of degeneration increases until a base level of fertility is reached. Because of this feature of land tenure, these systems are, in effect, self-destroying once the Critical Population Density has been exceeded.

In the case of short-fallow systems, with a small proportion of resting land, the fallow disappears very rapidly under population pressure. Continuous cultivation is possible, at least for a good many years, on the strong and fertile soils associated with these systems, and when this stage has been reached the individual rights inherent in cultivated land become very apparent. This symptom of decay was noted as a very unusual and remarkable example of 'customary individualization of tenure to a high degree' in the greatly over-crowded Kikuyu reserves of Kenya, where it facilitated the registration of individual titles.

Odd as it may seem, traditional communal tenure has not prohibited the emergence of African farming on a fairly large scale in some areas. The explanation is twofold. Individual rights extend over cultivated land however large the area, and relatively large areas can be acquired and held under customary rights provided that they are cultivated. It must be remembered that the plough and the work ox were unknown in sub-Saharan Africa before their recent introduction by Europeans. Acquisition of cultivated land was strictly limited by the capacity of the hand hoe and the labour power of the family. There was no need for explicit restrictions.

There are, however, limitations which affect the development and permanence of this type of farming, so long as traditional tenure forms survive. The land cannot be mortgaged or sold, and when it is transferred or vacated, particularly on the death of the operator, the rights of the owning lineage are likely to be asserted. Furthermore, the holding must consist wholly of cultivated crop land. As we have noted, all grazing land is commonage. The extent and nature of the rights in common grazing impose a strong restraint on pasture development and range management. Crop refuse too is common grazing. After harvest the farm must be opened to the flocks and herds of the community. These limitations on land use and tenure inhibit long-term investment and the development of permanently viable farming units.

In many developing countries the customary relations on which the systems of land tenure depend are losing their authority. People are becoming increasingly involved in impersonal contacts and contractual relations outside the closed community of clan and lineage. The result is discord and uncertainty. A change in the relationship between men and land is clearly due, but there is no consensus of opinion on the form this change should take and the types of tenure ultimately desired. After the Second World War there was quite a noticeable emergence of individualization, with sales of land, particularly in the case of land given over to permanent cash crops such as coffee and cocoa. In some cases even arable farmland was, in effect, sold under the fiction that the buyer was paying not for the land but the 'improvements'.

Many of the new African leaders, however, disapprove of the institution of private property in land. It is 'un-African'. There is a strong desire to preserve what is best in the old systems, the ideals of mutual help and social security. These, it is argued, can provide a basis for modern cooperative farming. This belief was also strongly held by many colonial administrators and agriculturists twenty years ago. Serious attempts were made to foster cooperative farming, particularly in Kenya, with no success at all. Others argue, equally convincingly, that individualization of land tenure is the only proven path to the development of economic farming. The view that both might have a place in the developing society receives little attention.

The communal tenure systems, the survival of traditional

values and the present uncertainties tend to keep production at a low level. So do very low incomes, general poverty with accompanying illiteracy, malnutrition and lethargy, and sheer inability to buy agricultural materials. The use of inputs such as fertilizers, insecticides and herbicides, better seed, irrigation water and farm power is, therefore, much less common than is the case in the next group of countries we shall consider.

DEVELOPING COUNTRIES WITH PRIVATE OWNERSHIP OF LAND

The relationships between men and land in this group of countries may be divided into three main categories: family smallholding systems with private ownership, tenancy systems and large-estate systems. These forms may operate side by side in the same country and, quite frequently, the last two have been transformed, or are being transformed, into the first by process of land reform. In many of these countries, agrarian reform, in the sense of a large-scale reallocation of rights in land, is a dominant issue.

Where the individually owned family smallholding is the rule, subdivision and fragmentation of land have usually reached a rather advanced stage. The former term denotes the splitting of holdings into smaller and smaller units, while 'fragmentation' refers to that condition in which the holding consists of a number of scattered parcels, irrespective of its aggregate size. Sub-division is an inevitable consequence of increase of the cultivator population beyond the critical point, where land is freely transferable and divisible. It is brought about by the pressures that reduce the fallow in the systems previously discussed: pressures arising from the imperative need for land as a means of livelihood. In the long-fallow systems the total size of the holding is reduced as population pressure increases. In this sense there is subdivision, but the reduction is at the expense of the fallow, at least until a very advanced stage is reached, and fragmentation is not a characteristic feature of this form of breakdown. Where all land is almost equally poor there is not much inducement to fragmentation. In the case of permanent and short-fallow systems, on the other hand—such as the cereal-fallow rotation of the Mediterranean and Near East—the cultivated area of the holding is reduced by subdivision at an early stage of population pressure, and fragmentation is characteristic. Similar features appear in African permanent and short-fallow systems on strong soils, as in Kikuyuland in Kenya and Chaggaland in Tanzania.

Fragmentation comes about, usually, as a result of efforts to share land equitably, in terms not only of area but of quality and suitability for different crops: to give fair shares in good, bad and indifferent land alike. Both processes are reinforced and sustained by social and legal sanctions or, in the case of Islamic observance, by religious precept. A man may will all of his land to one son but the claims of his other heirs are likely to be upheld by the courts, even when they are no longer justified by economic necessity.

In the more advanced stages of this dual process, the pattern of land holding degenerates into a confusion of rights in fragments of parcels, so diffuse that, very often, the rights cannot be exercised. At this stage there is a marked differentiation beween 'owned holdings' and 'operated holdings'; that is, between the aggregates of shares in parcels held by individuals and the areas which are worked as family 'farms'. The operated holding becomes an aggregate of scattered parcels some of which may be owned wholly or, more commonly, in part by the operator while others are held on a short-term agreement, generally share-cropping. This aggregate is also likely to contain parcels the ownership of which is in dispute, for as land rights become more diffuse they also become more indefinite. A recent investigation in a part of southern Anatolia, with which I was concerned, showed that the ownership of no less than 40 per cent of the area of agricultural land was in dispute. It was found that there were about 133000 operated holdings in the area under study and that these were composed of more than a million parcels in which well over two and a half million established land rights were vested. In this situation, the 'farm' unit is in a constant state of change by regrouping of parcels. There is no stability in the agrarian structure and the farmer has little security of tenure in the land he farms, even though the aggregate of his ownership rights may amount to a substantial number of hectares.

When population pressure is reduced by migration to

uncertain employment in the home country or temporary emigration abroad, as in Greece where movement to urban centres is combined with a marked migration of workers to Common Market countries, emigrants tend to retain their land rights and to lease them only on a short-term basis. Thus, while the average size of the operated holding is increased, at least temporarily, the differentiation between owned and operated holdings is accentuated and the stability of the agrarian structure is not improved.

Nevertheless, even a relatively advanced degree of subdivision does not prohibit the use of certain innovations, such as fertilizer practice, improved crop varieties and better seed, pesticides and herbicides and better cultural methods. Fragmentation does not prohibit their use but does make it more difficult and expensive in terms of time, transport and labour. Even a limited degree of heavy mechanization is possible, provided that parcels carrying the same crop are contiguous over a relatively large area and that cultivators cooperate in the use of machinery. On the other hand, water distribution and the economic development of new irrigation systems are often gravely impeded.

A number of countries, in which general poverty and its associated evils do not act as insuperable barriers, have achieved quite remarkable increases of productivity by a combination of these means. Japan is the superlative example. Most of these countries appear to have other features in common, including considerable advancement in industrial and urban development, a high standard of literacy among farmers, a previous history of agricultural research and reasonably adequate extension and cooperative services. Also, they are notably countries in which agrarian reforms have recently been completed. Titles to land are clear and definite and the pattern of holding has not degenerated into a confusion of multiple ownership and indefinite rights.

In these circumstances and by these means, the productivity of agriculture can be increased rapidly within the framework of a highly subdivided structure. There are, however, limitations to the process, as is demonstrated by the appearance of imbalance in the Japanese economy, with a lag in the growth-rate of agriculture, and in Greece by the accumulation of unmanageable surpluses combined with increasingly high levels of farm subsidies. The economies of scale cannot be achieved, products are often uncompetitive in the world market context, diversification is limited by the rigidity of the structure and, in spite of ingenuity and unremitting toil, the smallholding farmer remains poor in comparison with the city worker. Furthermore, although there may be some development of special enterprizes, general livestock husbandry tends to stand apart from these changes, to retain its traditional form and to remain static or decay.

Tenancy and sharecropping problems tend to arise in family-farm systems. In densely populated countries, typically in the Near and Far East, landlord–tenant problems become acute. The restraints on investment and productivity imposed by this system vary with the cultivator's security of tenure. He may be reasonably secure or he may be liable to lose his rights at very short notice. A more general restraint is the custom of sharecropping; the payment of a proportion of the harvest, often 50 per cent, rather than a fixed rent. The level of rent is also an important factor. It has been estimated that in Egypt, before the recent land reforms, over 60 per cent of the cultivated land was rented from middlemen on short-term leases at rentals that sometimes exceeded the net income from the land. The greater the pressure of population on the land the higher rents become, in cash or kind, and the less the cultivator can spend on farm materials and development. Landlords rarely, if ever, provide such materials, other than seed of doubtful quality, and the cultivator has little inducement to do so when he must bear the whole cost and give a share of the return.

Most developing countries with landlord–tenant systems have introduced measures of reform, mainly within the last decade or two. The simplest approach, it would seem, is to reform the tenancy system by regulating the conditions of contract, fixing levels of rental in cash or kind and requiring contracts to be put into writing. This has been done in Italy, the Philippines, China (Taiwan), a number of Latin American states and others, usually as a prelude to more comprehensive land reform. But the difficulties of enforcement have proved to be formidable or insuperable. The provision of an adequate inspectorate is beyond the capacity of most developing countries, particularly where population pressure is high and competition for tenancies intense.

Even in France, in 1963, it was found necessary to enact amending legislation designed to curb landlord evasion.

In some countries land is held in large units but the estates are farmed by the owners themselves, employing hired labour. We may call these 'large estate systems', to distinguish them from the landlord–tenant systems. They vary in form and present different problems. Where plantations are efficiently managed and the management employs and keeps abreast of modern methods, no problems of productivity arise. But efficient plantations are often foreign owned and this may give rise to local hostility and transfer of ownership, either voluntarily as in Malaysia and Guatemala or by expropriation as in Cuba. Such transfers serve national, social and political ends but often result in decreased productivity. Where plantations of this type are owned by nationals, social problems arise from inequalities of wealth and income. These are often dealt with by legislation designed to protect and improve the condition of the workers and to strengthen their bargaining power.

Acute problems of productivity arise where the operation of large-estate systems is based on static and highly inefficient forms of extensive land use, with dependent and servile labour. Social problems are no less acute, particularly where the labour-extensive system cannot absorb a growing population and increasing numbers are forced to live in poverty on totally inadequate plots of marginal land. Such was the situation in many Latin American countries until comparatively recently, and it persists in some. It is a situation which calls for drastic measures of reform if an explosive and revolutionary solution is to be avoided.

LAND REFORM

In the last two decades there has been a spate of land reforms, in the sense of redistribution of farm property between large estates and peasant farms or among peasant farms of various sizes. In the past, change of this sort was primarily a product of war or revolution or both. More recently, it has come to be regarded as a preventive rather than an aftermath of revolution; as a means of ensuring political and social stability. Most reforms, however, have been carried out as emergency measures with varying motivations. The general objectives include, almost invariably, 'social justice' and appeasement of the peasantry by reducing the concentration of land, wealth and income. Sometimes the process has been stimulated and complicated by the need to resettle a large displaced population, and political motives, although usually unproclaimed, often play an important part. The concept of land reform in relation to productivity, as a prerequisite for economic advance, has received less attention. In most cases, expediency has been the dominant consideration. Consequently, there is as yet no adequate body of theory, or set of generalizations, whereby reforms may be guided and evaluated.

Land tenure reform raises productivity only to the extent that it creates conditions conducive to, and is followed by, operational reform. In many cases, where political and social considerations have been dominant, productivity and resource allocation have been virtually ignored, or considered only passively by exempting efficient estates from subdivision. Grave difficulties of implementation are commonly encountered and these may be complicated by reaction of one sort or another. Consequently, the effect on productivity has often been at best limited and at worst negative.

The impact of the reforms in India has been very limited. Major difficulties have been encountered in grading land and fixing area ceilings, determining compensation and financing land purchase, and above all, in countering evasion by fictitious transfer. Syria and Iraq have met with similar difficulties accentuated by lack of land records, acute shortage of administrative resources, and, in Iraq, by uncertainty as to the final form of tenure desired. Consequently, expropriation of land, and to an even greater extent redistribution, lag far behind schedule. In Iraq, most of the land so far expropriated is still held by the state and leased to cultivators under collective tenancy agreements. These delays and uncertainties inhibit development and retard investment, even by landlords in land they might expect to retain. A particularly difficult problem is that of replacing the managerial and entrepreneurial functions of the landlords. Cooperative organization is usually seen as the answer to this problem but in many developing countries such organizations do not as yet have the managerial skills or the resources to operate effectively.

Practically all of the recent reforms have reduced the concentration of ownership but they have also subdivided the land into many units too small to be economically viable or to yield more than a meagre living. The Mexican reform, for example, increased the proportion of landowners from three per cent to 50 per cent of the rural population, but nearly 85 per cent of the holdings, occupying 74 per cent of the land, are less than five hectares. Most of the occupants of such holdings remain in dire need, at income levels barely sufficient for subsistence. By their own efforts they can do little or nothing to improve productivity. Such is the situation also in Bolivia and other states of Latin America where land reform has not as yet had any positive economic effect.

In a few countries, however, land reform has been accompanied by, and may have been partly responsible for, a marked increase of agricultural productivity. These are countries in which reform has not been regarded as an end in itself and direct measures have been taken to deal with problems of land operation and productivity. We have already noted the examples of Japan and Greece and the circumstances which facilitated the effective application of new inputs in these countries, in spite of their highly subdivided agrarian structures. We have also noted the limitation of this form of development. The United Arab Republic may be added to the list, although it is a country of tiny holdings. After the Egyptian reforms 95 per cent of owners had less than two hectares, and half of these had less than half a hectare. But here too there were favourable circumstances; not least, the extraordinary qualities of the Nile Valley lands. Before the reforms, productivity per acre was higher than in Britain. Reform, as an aftermath of revolution, was facilitated by the existence of a developed land registration system and a well-trained administration, and by the fact that the area concerned was relatively small and manageable. Urbanization and industrialization were not inconsiderable. There was a legacy of agricultural research, and technical innovations had been introduced. On the other hand, peasant techniques were primitive, levels of literacy, skill and efficiency were low, and many of the new farmers were former landless labourers. To offset these restraints on productivity, land-use cooperatives were established and membership was made compulsory for recipients of land. In effect, individual holdings were pooled for cropping purposes, and for administration of credit, and were placed under skilled direction and government supervision. Various forms of pooled marketing were tried out, with success where sufficiently skilled management could be provided. The effects of the reduced scale of operations was offset by these means, and productivity increased. But the over-all result is by no means attributable to land reallocation alone. Reduction and control of rents affected a much greater proportion of the land and were accompanied by a general increase in the use of fertilizers to which the improvement of productivity may be largely attributable. Although the economic effects of these reforms may be counted as positive, great inequalities of wealth remain and the peasant on his tiny holding still lives at an income level little above bare subsistence.

In China (Taiwan) limited measures of reform have been accompanied by a marked increase in agricultural productivity and in rural standards of living. Here, the rental system was reformed and a ceiling placed on ownership of rented land, but no limit was imposed on the size of the operated holding. Many favourable factors contributed to this success, including a high literacy level among farmers, a long tradition of local cooperation, an influx of technical and administrative skills from Mainland China, and technical guidance, ample credit and generous grants and subsidies made possible by external aid. In the Philippines, too, reform started with an adjustment of landlord–tenant relations but this is to be followed by a second phase of land reallocation accompanied by a programme of intensive agricultural and community development employing large teams of technical workers. The programme has been delayed by shortage of trained staff, difficulties of training and the working out of administrative procedures.

DEVELOPED COUNTRIES WITH PRIVATE OWNERSHIP OF LAND

No country has succeeded in ridding its agriculture altogether of excessively small and fragmented units, but Britain and the Soviet Union have gone a long way towards achieving this end. They did so by very different means neither of which has much in common with the classic types of land reform. In Britain it was a long and evolutionary process, which, in the end, allowed economic forces to determine the size distribution of production units: in the Soviet Union, on the other hand, the tenure system was abruptly changed and regulated in accordance with the economic philosophy of Marxian socialism. Indeed, it is doubtful if the Soviet Union should be included, for the collective farm does not so much remove as conceal the fact of land subdivision.

Most of the developed industrial countries of Western Europe are still burdened with a legacy of subdivided and fragmented farmland. In these countries there has been a recent, and very significant, decrease in the number of farms with a concomitant increase of farm size. Yet in the Netherlands 40 per cent of all farms are still less than five hectares and 65 per cent are less than 10 hectares. In France, 30 per cent are less than five hectares and 50 per cent less than 10 hectares. In Italy, 75 per cent are less than 10 hectares, and the majority of farms in the Federal German Republic are also in this category. France has about 16 million hectares and West Germany nearly 11 million hectares of fragmented farmland.

These countries are engaged in 'land reform' in reverse, in an earnest endeavour to increase the concentration of land ownership and operation. The European Economic Community, to which they belong, recognizes that this situation presents one of its most pressing agrarian problems and has established a central fund to finance the structural reform of agriculture throughout the Community. Member states also have their own funds and all have adopted more or less radical measures to hasten the process of farm amalgamation and the development of larger and more efficient production units. These measures include retirement pensions for older farmers who give up their land, vocational training schemes and grants for younger farmers and farm workers who are willing to work in other industries, quittance grants and other financial inducements to leave the land, grants and loans to encourage movement of farmers from overcrowded to less crowded areas, and generous credit terms to meet the cost of amalgamating uneconomic units with others. Some countries have special measures of their own, including the formation of joint farming groups in France and, in Italy, compulsory acquisition of land for farm enlargement and valuable tax exemptions for farmers who buy land to enlarge their holdings. All of these countries have programmes of land reallocation to increase farm size, consolidation and reclamation of land where these measures are necessary, and the extension of farm utility services and facilities.

Britain has no great problem of fragmented farmland but she too has been left with some legacy of subdivision, in relation to the economic conditions of today. The proportion of small farmers of less than 50 acres (20 hectares) whose net return is lower than the statutory wage of an agricultural labourer has been cited as the main cause of agricultural inefficiency. As a well-known farmer-writer, A. G. Street, has put it, the small farmer is no longer the backbone of British agriculture but the slipped disc. In the United States also the number of farmers is well above the economic optimum. It has been argued that the continuing demand for price supports for agriculture is due to the existence of too many small producers who cannot prosper as farmers because of shortage of land and capital, and that the only real remedy is more city jobs. The spectacular rise in farm productivity achieved in the United States, as in Britain, in recent decades did not come from improved technologies alone but from a combination of improved technologies, heavy capital investment and larger production units. In the decade 1950–9, the number of farms in the United States decreased by 31 per cent and the average size of farm increased by 40 per cent. In Iraq, in the same period, the number of farms increased by 102 per cent and the average size of farm decreased by 38 per cent.

In western Europe as a whole, agricultural production has continued to increase rapidly over the last decade, mainly as a result of higher yields and more efficient production units. The increase in livestock output due to larger herds and better breeding and feeding has been particularly striking.

CENTRALLY PLANNED ECONOMIES

In the Soviet plan of development the highest priority was given to expansion of heavy industry, at the expense of increased production of food and other consumer goods. This approach was possible because at the beginning of the revolution the country was producing a substantial agricultural surplus. The first land tenure reforms were designed to equalize the distribution of land among cultivators: they prohibited both private ownership and tenancy. The effect was to destroy the larger and more efficient production units from which the surplus had largely been drawn and to necessitate an abrupt reversal of policy. Tenancy, wage labour and private farming were restored for a time. This emergency measure was followed by a period of intensive collectivization, during which agriculture remained the Achilles heel of the Soviet economy. The object, according to Stalin, was 'to turn the small and scattered peasant farms into larger united farms based on the common cultivation of the soil'. It was not an easy process. Harsh and repressive measures were necessary to collect and direct the flow of the meagre surplus, to limit consumption, especially by the farmers themselves, and to prevent the cultivators reaping the main benefits of increased production.

Nevertheless, the socialization of the economy did have certain positive effects on agriculture. Mechanization and investment were increased and total output expanded. The composition of the agricultural product changed in response to the needs of industry, and rural under-employment was to some extent reduced by transfer of labour. But the land–labour ratio increased only slowly. Even in 1961, some 38 per cent of the USSR's labour force was still employed in agriculture.

Important institutional changes have taken place, mainly in the last decade, and are still in progress. Before the Second World War, the average collective farm (kolkhoz) was a group of eighty-one families farming 492 hectares, or six hectares per family. By 1963, the programme of amalgamation which started in 1952 had increased the size of the average collective to 411 families farming 2896 hectares. This resulted in some benefits of scale but the land–labour ratio was only slightly increased, to seven hectares per family. Expedients such as the collective obscure but do not greatly alter the fundamental facts of land subdivision. A much more significant change in the tenure pattern is the rapid growth of the far less labour intensive sovkhoz (state farm) at the expense of the kolkhoz. In 1954, the state farms held 12 per cent of the agricultural land but by 1963 this had increased to over 50 per cent, and in the same period the average size of the sovkhoz trebled. It is now a very large unit with, on the average, 10000 hectares of sown area and a labour force of 775 workers. According to Russian leaders, the state farm system has proved more effective than collective farming and the ultimate objective appears to be a streamlined agricultural organization under which all farm workers will become state employees like their brothers in industry. In the Communist doctrine this is 'the highest form of socialist agriculture'.

The same tendencies are noticeable in the eastern European countries with centrally-planned economies, except Poland which abandoned collectivization. The average size of the collective farm has increased very sharply, but only in Bulgaria has it reached, and even exceeded, that of the Soviet kolkhoz. The number of state farms is also increasing, but the change. from collective to state farming is less rapid than in the USSR.

The effects of these recent changes cannot be assessed with any accuracy because adequate comparative data for Eastern Europe and the USSR are not available. Gross agricultural output has undoubtedly increased rapidly in the last decade, at an over-all rate comparable with that of Western Europe, but it has generally fallen short of the planned targets. A large part of the increase took place in the first half of the present decade and appears to have come from the opening up of new land, in particular, the vast area of virgin lands in the USSR, rather than improved efficiency and yields. This involved the ploughing up of uncultivated lands in Siberia and Khazakstan as great in extent as the whole arable acreage of Canada. It was, in effect, a reallocation of land resources from tribal herding to cultivation. At the same time there was a reallocation of land between crops, in response to industrial needs and changing consumer demand. The areas under industrial crops, vegetables, orchards, plantations, vineyards and fodder crops expanded while the food grain area declined. Apparently, the area sown to food grains fell below the level required to meet the country's needs in a very adverse season. Such a season came in 1962/3 and in the following year the USSR's imports of grain were so great as to reduce world wheat stocks to their lowest level since 1953.

It is now generally realized that the world's food balance is extremely precarious and that there is a widening gap between the richer and the poorer countries. In 1965/6, according to FAO estimates, food production *per caput* in the developing areas dropped back to the 1957/8 level. Only in West Europe and America was there any increase.

In general, land tenure systems as such are neutral in relation to productivity, but the forces which give rise to agrarian decay operate through them. The most powerful of these forces is population pressure. In long-fallow systems under communal tenure, population pressure leads to reduction of the fallow and decline of fertility; in family smallholding systems with private ownership, to intense subdivision and fragmentation of land; in landlord–tenant systems, to an increasing rent spiral; in large-estate systems, to reallocation of land and excessive subdivision; in collective and cooperative systems, to hidden subdivision. No tenure system can resist the effects of this force. Those of the developed countries appear to do so only because industrialization and diversification of their economies has diverted pressure from the land.

One of the principal indicators of a country's level of economic development is the distribution of population between agriculture and the rest of the economy. It might be stated almost as a general rule that national living standards are inversely proportional to the ratio of employment in agriculture and in other sectors. The developing countries, as a whole, employ some 80 per cent of their total labour force in producing the nation's food supplies and other soil products. In the countries of advanced development less than 20 per cent suffices, and this small proportion produces better products in much greater quantity. About 120 man-hours of work are required to produce a quintal of grain by African methods against two to four man-hours on the modern advanced farm.

Agriculture's share of the world labour force is declining. This is a general tendency, but in other respects there is a very significant difference between the developed and the developing countries. In the developed countries the absolute size of the agricultural population is also declining. In the developing countries, on the other hand, the agricultural population and the number of workers employed on the land continues to increase in absolute terms. The rate of shift from agriculture is determined by the relation between the absolute increase in the volume of non-agricultural employment and the absolute numbers added to the work force by population growth in the same period. In almost all the industrial countries this ratio has been growing fast enough to produce a continuing decline of the population employed on the land. The shift has been accompanied, both in the capitalist and communist nations, by more intensive capitalization of agriculture, growth of the farm unit and greater efficiency of production. In most of the less developed countries the reverse is the case. Population increase rates are high and the ratio of the growth rate of non-agricultural employment to that of the work force is decreasing. Once the critical point has been passed, the agrarian structures crumble under the impact of continuing pressure of population on the land. In these circumstances, population growth itself produces conditions which make the problems of agricultural development and food supply almost despairingly difficult. This is one of the main reasons why agriculture has so often failed to play the part it should in the transition from stagnant to expanding economies.

CHAPTER 8

THE RESOURCES OF AGRICULTURE

by J. B. Hutchinson

INTRODUCTION

The natural resources by which the needs of human communities for food are met, comprise climate and soil and those plants and animals that have been domesticated to give the crops and livestock of the world's farming systems. On climate, man's influence has been limited to the provision of housing for himself and livestock, and glass housing for some specialist high value crops. On soils, fertility improvement has contributed very largely to the high productivity of the agriculture of advanced human communities. It has been on those plant and animal species that man has domesticated, however, that he has achieved the greatest impact, though with the whole range of the plant and animal kingdoms to choose from, he has selected only a very small number of species for exploitation.

The foodstuffs produced from domesticated plant species, or crop plants, fall largely, but not entirely, into four broad categories:

(1) *Grains:* primarily energy sources and secondarily protein sources. Most, but not all, of the world's grain comes from cereal crops of the grass family.

(2) *Oilseeds:* primarily concentrated energy sources, and secondarily protein sources. Oilseeds are produced by a wide range of botanical species.

(3) *Pulses:* primarily protein sources, and secondarily energy sources. Pulses are produced entirely by plants of the family Leguminosae.

(4) *Root crops:* energy sources, very low in protein. Root crops embrace a wide range of plant species.

There are, of course, food crops that lie outside these categories. The most important are the vegetables from which minerals and vitamins are obtained, beverages and stimulants such as cacao, tea and coffee, and such energy sources as the sugar-producing plants and the starchy bananas of the tropics. Moreover, there is a large and important category of industrial crops that are not grown for their contribution to the food supply; rubber, cotton, dyestuffs, and timber.

It is known, from such evidence as the food stores of early man that have been discovered, and the stomach contents of corpses preserved in peat bogs, that a wider range of plants was exploited at the beginnings of agriculture than has survived in modern crops. Some plants were domesticated and grown for a time, but were given up when the superior potential of the ancestors of our more successful crop plants became apparent. So, the basic range of crops on which our agriculture has been built was a narrow one. This was at least partly because agriculture developed from very few original foci. The best known and certainly the most important foci were two that have been found in rather dry open woodland savannah country, one in the headwaters of the Euphrates and Tigris in the Old World, and one in semi-arid lowland Mexico in the New World. It is on the results of the exploitation of the climate, soils, flora and fauna of these two areas that agriculture is based, and in all its subsequent spread the systems there developed for the exploitation of climate and soil, and the plants and animals there domesticated, have dominated agricultural practice.

CROPS AND STOCK

When agriculture began in the headwaters of the Euphrates and Tigris, the first farmers lived in open country, with grasslands in the lower and drier areas and woodlands in the higher and moister regions. To the south were the desert plains of Mesopotamia, and to the north and west were grasslands and forests stretching across Turkey to the Mediterranean and the Danube, and up into western Europe. An important stimulus to the development of agriculture was the need to harvest and store some form of food for the winter season, and there were to hand several species of grass that grew in abundance, ripened in the summer, and produced seed that could be stored and drawn upon as it was needed. So the grasses provided grain, a ready source of storable food that kept the community supplied from one growing season to the next. By selection under cultivation, improved strains better adapted to growth under cultivation were isolated, and the first cereals, barleys and wheats, came into being. Grasses were not the only source of grain. Some broad-leaved plants, such as *Chenopodium* were grown for their grain early in the history of agriculture. The grasses proved superior, however, and while the broad leaved plants grown for grain soon declined or disappeared, other grasses were added to the range of cereals. Communities moving westward added oats and rye to the original barley and wheat. Those who moved south adopted sorghum, bulrush millet and finger millet in Africa. Those who migrated southeast and took agriculture to India added rice, one of the greatest cereals, to the range of grain crops.

Two other plant families made contributions of very great importance to the list of crop plants of the Old World. Among the Cruciferae the genus *Brassica* has given rise to an enormous range of food plants. *Brassica* species have been domesticated as oilseeds in central Asia, India, and the Mediterranean region. Rai, sarson and toria are important Asiatic crops contributing substantially to the vegetable oil supplies of India. Rape seed is an old established European oilseed, grown as far north as Sweden. In the Mediterranean and western Europe, root crops such as turnips, swedes and kohl rabi have been bred, also from *Brassica* species. And the green vegetable markets of the temperate regions of the world are supplied with cabbages, brussels sprouts, kale, cauliflowers, broccoli and the like, all from the genus *Brassica*.

Like the Gramineae, the Brassicas supply calories, but the Brassicas supply also vitamins and minerals in green vegetables. They all supply some protein, but a richer source of vegetable protein was exploited by the domestication of species of the third great crop plant family, the Leguminosae. From these, the legumes, came peas and beans, used both as green vegetables and as dry, high protein, seeds. In Europe the broad bean and the horse bean, and peas are among the old established crops. In India, besides peas a wide range of leguminous species has been domesticated to yield lentils and grams. In Africa the cow pea (*Vigna*), lubia (*Dolichos*), and minor crops such as the Bambara groundnut were added to the list of cultivars.

These three families provided the ancestors of the most important crop plants of the Old World, but other families have also been used. In the Chenopodiaceae the wild beet of coastal

Europe gave rise to beetroot, spinach beet, and more recently sugar beet. The Eurasian *Linum* gave the fibre flax and the oil seed, linseed, and the Afro-Indian species of *Gossypium* gave the cottons of the Old World.

Animal protein in the form of meat was of major importance in man's hunting days, before the origin of agriculture. The domestication of animals appears to have started at much the same time as the growing of crops, and made possible the transition from hunting to farming without a fall in dietary values. The earliest domestic animals were the sheep, goats and cattle of the regions in which agriculture was first practised. Pigs were added from the woodlands, and horses from the grass plains of eastern Europe and western Asia. As farming peoples spread they added new crops to their repertoire, but they did not greatly enlarge their list of domestic animals. Water buffaloes were domesticated in the wet lands of Asia, and camels in the deserts, but the only major addition to man's domestic livestock as he moved eastwards in the Old World was the Asiatic jungle fowl.

Agriculture developed independently, and at about the same time, in the dry lowlands of Mexico. There also the Gramineae and the Leguminosae provided the main sources of cultivated plants. America developed only one cereal, but that, maize, has become one of the world's great sources of human food. As in the Old World, some broad leaved plants were domesticated as grains, and species of *Chenopodium* and *Amaranthus* are still grown on a small scale, but the dominance of the cereal, maize, is virtually complete. Among the legumes, three species of *Phaseolus* were domesticated in Central America, and one in Peru. *Arachis*, the groundnut, was domesticated probably in what is now northern Argentina. These became the major New World sources of vegetable protein. *Brassica* is an Old World genus, and was not available to the beginners of New World agriculture, but to some extent its place as a source of vegetables has been taken by the *Cucurbitaceae*, from which have come the squashes and pumpkins.

Livestock were quite unimportant in indigenous New World agriculture—the turkey, the guinea pig, and the Andean cameloids were the only domesticates, comparable in importance only with such minor Old World acquisitions as the guinea fowl and the rabbit.

Since the most important centres of origin of agriculture were in open grassy country, most of the major crops are ecologically adapted to the climates that give rise to a grassland climax. Not all crop plants were domesticated in these regions, however, and the domesticates of two other climatic regions, the circumtropical lowland forests, and the highlands of the South American Andes, must be noted. Tropical forest food crops include the pantropical yams, the sweet potatoes and manioc of tropical America, and the bananas of south-east Asia. From the forest regions come a range of tree crops such as coffee, cacao, oil palm and coconuts. In the high Andes the potatoes were domesticated, together with species of *Tropaeolum* and *Oxalis*, and a *Chenopodium* grain.

Domestication of both crops and stock was complete before the dawn of history, and most species have undergone such rapid and extensive evolutionary change as to be very widely distinct from their wild ancestors. The course and genetic nature of the changes that have gone on have been extensively studied, and the evolutionary history of many crop plants is now well known. Briefly, the changes under domestication have involved first, increases in the size and the numbers of the parts of the plant useful to man, and secondly changes in the habit of growth of the plant that increase its suitability to crop production. The size of grains and size of ears in cereals and the size of seeds and of pods in legumes have been increased by the same kinds of selective process as have given rise to the large fleshy root of the turnip, the grotesquely hypertrophied inflorescence of the cauliflower, or the great fleshy fruit of the pumpkin and the squash. These are lines of development on which it was natural for man to breed his crops, and one can see the same selective process in operation in the abandonment of *Amaranthus*, with its multitude of minute grains, in favour of maize, with fewer but larger and more useful seeds.

Changes in plant habit are not so obviously related to the selective forces of domestication, but increasingly the study of crop physiology has revealed their adaptive significance. Smartt's studies in Cambridge of the New World beans of the genus *Phaseolus* have shown that the process of domestication led to the evolution from multibranched scrambling perennials, first of simple, unbranched climbing forms and then of dwarf bush types, that are much more easily managed in crop culture. These simple climbers and bush types, moreover, produced a much higher proportion of their dry weight as seeds, and they were not so long lived. It is apparent that such factors are inter-related. A simple unbranched plant is not well adapted to re-growth after the end of a season, and a plant in which the greater part of the resources are devoted to seed production is likely to lack the reserves for the repeated re-growth of a perennial. This evolutionary pattern is very common throughout the range of crop plants. Productivity in modern cereals has been increased by shifting the proportion between vegetative and seed production in favour of the latter. In sorghum it is possible to study the whole range from the wild grass of the African savannahs to the advanced cultivars of modern American agriculture. The wild grass is a slender, much branched, annual or semi-perennial with small heads and small seeds. Related to this, and still inter-crossing with it, is a great range of African cultivated races, larger and with larger heads and seeds, less branched, and each adapted to grow vegetatively for the whole rainy season of its area before producing a fruiting head. Only with the selection of less vegetative types, fruiting early regardless of the season, has really high production been attained, and in the single stalked, dwarf, large-seeded, heavy panicled American races the proportion of vegetative matter to grain has been reduced to the lowest level.

In genetic terms, these changes have gone on by selection in highly variable populations, the great variability having been carried in the vast populations that are generated under domestication. Major advances have come about through the selection of a few major genes, as with maize, or by the accumulation of numerous genes of small individual effect, as with the annual habit of the modern cottons. Polyploidy has been important in crops such as wheat, oats, and sugar-cane. It has played no part in others, as for example barley, maize, and beans. In fact every known genetic resource has been exploited in the improvement of one crop or another, and the evolutionary genetics of crop plants is among the most instructive studies of modern times.

Considering the very limited repertoire of crop plants, one must enquire whether there are prospects of improving agricultural potential by a wider range of domestications. Only one important crop has been added to agriculture in historic times, and that is *Hevea* rubber. Seed was brought from Brazil and seedlings established in Ceylon and Malaya in the late nineteenth century. There they gave rise to the plantation rubber crops of commerce. Although *Hevea* is a large tree with a long generation time, already there have arisen under selection stocks of widely different and superior performance, and adaptation to the conditions of agricultural production has been improved. In short, in a very few generations the *Hevea* rubber tree has become a crop plant. There is therefore no great difficulty to be anticipated in undertaking further domestications if the need arises. The need has not arisen. There is a sufficiency of crops for human needs, and the crops now in cultivation are so far in advance of their own wild ancestors that the chance of producing from another wild plant something good enough to supplement any of them is extremely remote.

The scope for further domestication is probably greater in the animal than in the plant kingdom. Pigs and poultry are not difficult to feed in any climate of the world, provided the agriculture is sufficiently advanced to produce a surplus of the kinds of crops that provide human food. Cereals, beans, and oilseed wastes can be used to make up pig and poultry rations, once human requirements have been met. Ruminant livestock, on the other hand, require high quality forage for efficient production. This is best provided by the grasses and clovers of temperate region grasslands. The grasslands of the tropics carry less nutritious species, and on the whole the period of the year over which they provide useful stock feed is short. The large mammals of tropical grasslands supplement their grazing extensively by browsing, and there is good reason to believe that a properly managed mixed savannah would best be exploited by stock that would browse as well as graze. Some of the African antelopes can be tamed readily, and there would seem to be scope for improving the meat supply, of Africa particularly, by running herds of tame antelopes.

These are the resources of agriculture in crops and stock. They are under man's full control. The more they are developed and adapted to man's needs the less their prospects of survival without him. Highly selected crops must be harvested, stored, and sown in clean land or they die out. Only more primitive forms, often hybridizing with related wild species, survive in land abandoned from cultivation. Domestic animals are likewise at a disadvantage in the wild. In favourable circumstances unspecialized stocks have indeed established themselves, as for example Spanish horses in the New World, and goats on some oceanic islands. With more advanced races this is no longer possible. The capacity to hatch her eggs and mother her chicks has been bred out of the modern hen. The dairy cow produces so much milk that, even with her calf to suckle, she would succumb to udder ills if she were not regularly milked.

CLIMATE AND SOIL

The three major variable components of the natural environment of agriculture are energy, water and soil. Energy, ultimately of solar origin, determines light and temperature, and hence the conditions of plant growth and of animal comfort. The relation of the earth to the sun is such that a very large part of the world's land mass has a cold season in which plant growth is slowed down, or ceases altogether. Man has no control, and no prospect of control, over the incidence of solar radiation, and the pattern of distribution of temperature and day length over the world is one which must be accepted as we find it. He can, and does, influence the effects of light and temperature on his crops and stock by housing.

Over water supplies man gained a measure of control early in the history of agriculture, in that he learnt how to supplement by irrigation from rivers the inadequacy of the rainfall in arid lands. This is a form of control that is only possible where rivers drawing water from a more favourable rainfall regime run through country where there is a water deficit.

The needs of plants for water are determined by the physical relation between energy supply and water evaporation. Of the energy received by a plant from the sun, a small proportion is used in photosynthesis. The rest is dissipated in the evaporation of water, either from the soil surface or by transpiration from the plant. This total evaporative loss is referred to as evapotranspiration. The amount of water a crop needs is proportionate to the amount of energy to be dissipated. Crop water requirements are greatest in hot arid climates where the sun always shines.

They are least in cool, damp, cloudy climates where much of the incident radiation is cut off by the moisture laden atmosphere. In hot arid climates it is necessary to supply water in large quantities if crops are to be grown. For example, at Wad Medani in the Sudan, it is normal practice to supply by irrigation, water equivalent to a 1250 mm rainfall to a cotton crop that is only in the ground for nine months. By contrast, in England water shortage arises primarily from irregularities in rainfall distribution and not from inadequacy in total amount, and 600 mm of rain in Cambridge is sufficient for good crop growth and some run off to rivers.

It is within the range of about 500 mm to 1250 mm that rain- ←
fall and crop water requirement are most commonly in balance. In Figs. 9, 10 and 11 are given world maps of average annual precipitation, approximate crop land area, and world population. It will be seen that there is little crop land and a very sparse human population in the world's deserts, and what there is, is confined to river valleys where irrigation is possible. Equally important is the absence of crop land, and of human populations, from most of the heavy rainfall areas of the world. Annual precipitation in excess of 1500 mm is confined to the tropics, and to narrow belts on mountainous windward coasts of temperate regions. The major areas of heavy rainfall, the wet tropical regions, now mostly covered with rain forest, are often supposed to constitute a large reserve of potential agricultural land. They are areas where there is an excess of precipitation over the amount that can be disposed of by evapotranspiration. This excess water either runs off or percolates through the soil to the water table. Either way, the productive potential of the land is reduced. When water runs off it takes soil with it, and erosion results. Good soil is carried away, and good land is scored with gullies and ravines. Percolation, on the other hand, results in the soluble nutrients in the soil being washed away and the fertility of the soil is consequently reduced. Natural climax vegetation minimizes these losses. A good root mat, either forest roots or grass roots, holds the soil and run off is of clear water. Mineral nutrients locked up in living plants or undecayed dead vegetation are not leached away, and hence a mature vegetative cover may live indefinitely by turning over a small supply of mineral nutrients, most of which is at any one time locked up in organic

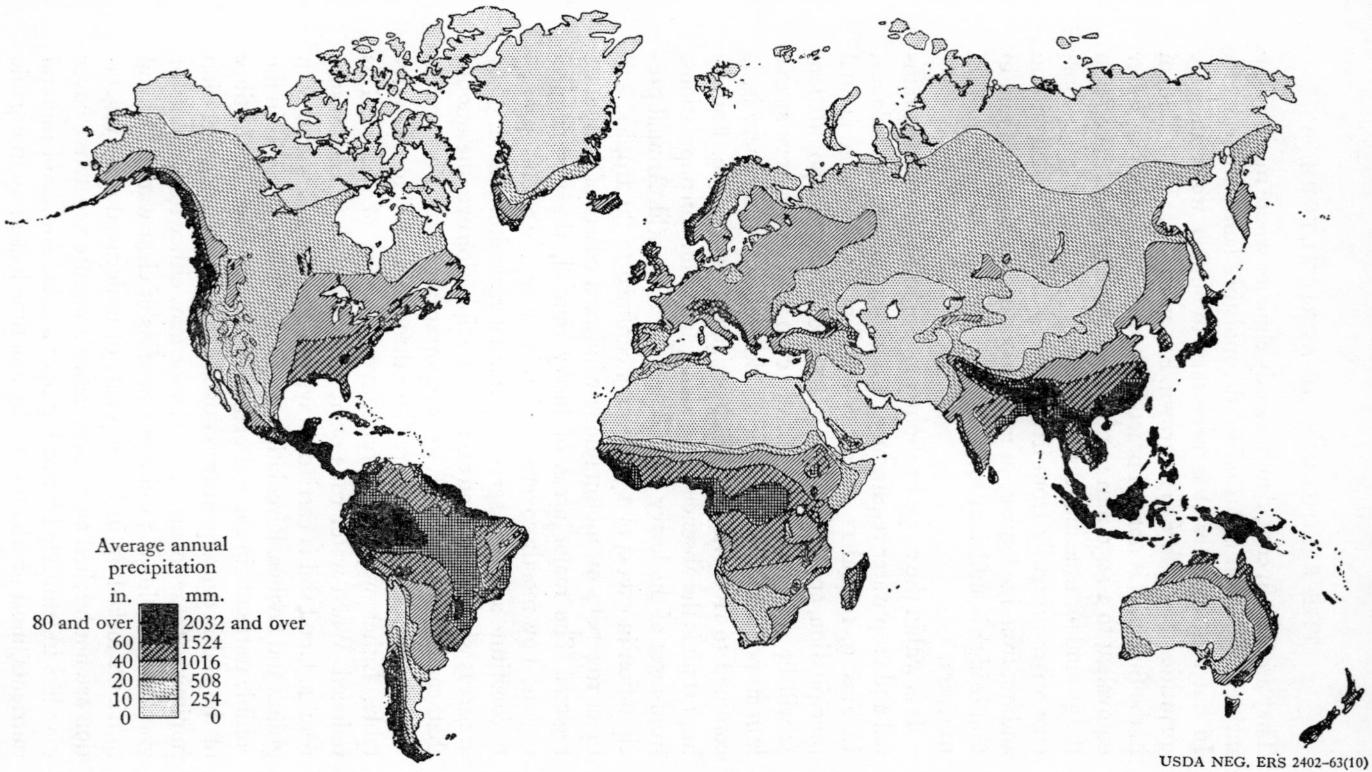
Average annual
precipitation
in. mm.
80 and over 2032 and over
60 1524
40 1016
20 508
10 254
0 0
USDA NEG. ERS 2402-63(10)

Fig. 9 The World: average annual rainfall. (USDA).

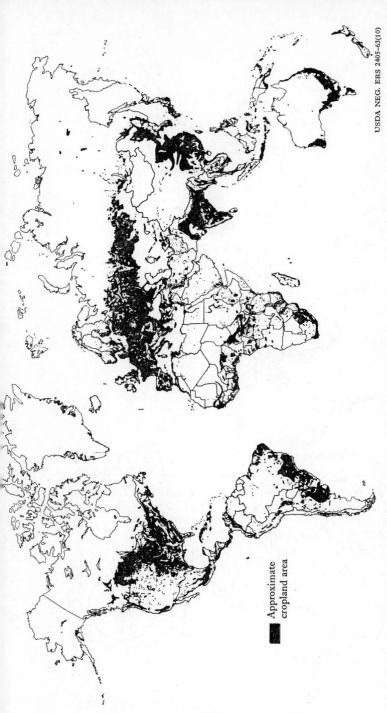

Approximate
cropland area

Fig. 10   The World: distribution of cropland area. Arable, including fallow, tree and bush crops. (USDA). Partly because sufficiently detailed data on land use are not available for some countries and partly because the map is small, the shaded portions include scattered areas of land not used for crops and the unshaded portion scattered cropland areas.

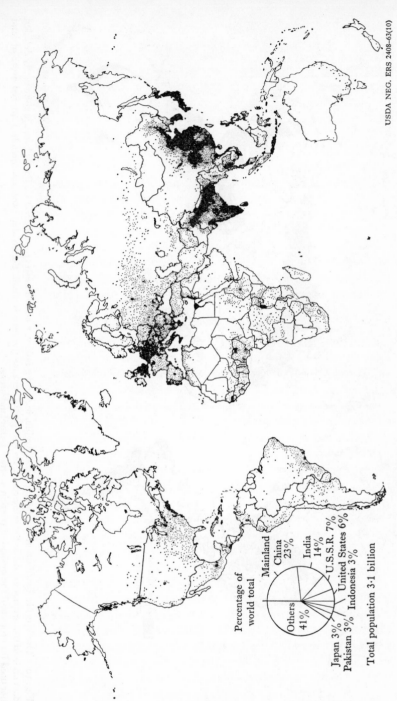

Percentage of
world total

Mainland
China
23%

India
14%

U.S.S.R. 7%

United States 6%

Indonesia 3%

Japan 3%

Pakistan 3%

Others
41%

Total population 3·1 billion

USDA NEG. ERS 2408–63(10)

Fig. 11   The World: distribution of human population, 1961. (USDA). Each dot represents 200000 persons.

matter. This stable situation comes to an end when the land is cleared for agriculture. On first clearing and at regular intervals in the cropping cycle, the soil is exposed, the nutrient supply is mobilized in inorganic form in the soil for the benefit of the following crop, and the whole system is vulnerable to erosion and leaching.

For this reason the regions of the earth where rainfall is substantially in excess of evaporative requirement are unpromising agriculturally. Soils are poor, since nutrients beyond those locked up in the living cycle have long since been washed away. This is so whether it be on the Welsh mountains with moderate rainfall and low evaporation, or the Amazon valley where although evaporation is high it is greatly exceeded by the rainfall. Short term cropping is exploitive and destructive, and for permanent agriculture it is necessary to depend on permanent vegetation, and on building up a living system that will both retain a reserve of nutrients in the living cycle and at all times protect the soil against erosion. This is achieved in the wetter parts of the temperate region by maintaining a permanent sward and gaining a return from livestock products. Small and repeated applications of nutrients are necessary if the forage crop is to be improved without incurring substantial waste of nutrients by leaching.

In rain forest country, so far the chief permanent form of agriculture is the growing of tree crops, or of a semi-perennial like sugar cane. Plantation agriculture of this kind supports only a small human population, and there is little scope for the development of food crop farming such as would provide a satisfactory livelihood for large human communities. Tropical climates with a heavy rainfall do not therefore offer scope for development beyond that necessary to satisfy the needs of temperate regions for tropical plantation crops.

The one exception to the generalization that heavy rainfall areas can only be maintained permanently in agriculture with tree crops, is rice culture. Rice can be grown in standing water, and hence is grown under circumstances where the rainfall may be greatly in excess of crop water use. The land must, however, be laid out in level fields in order that there may be a uniform depth of water throughout. Fields may be large on level plains, or very small on terraced slopes. Erosion is prevented, since the water moves only slowly. Leaching is usually unimportant, as the field is puddled, and there is little percolation. Indeed, since much of the water is run-off from higher lands, some increment of fertility accrues to the rice lands from the products of erosion.

In the arid lands all the major areas to which irrigation water can be brought have already been developed, and further extensions of irrigation will only add marginally to the world's crop land. In the wet lands, the problems involved in establishing productive arable agriculture have so far proved insuperable, except in the rice cultures of Asia. Thus the contribution of the wet lands to the extension of world's cropland is also likely to be marginal. In the medium rainfall areas, the greater part of that suitable as cropland has already been developed, but some reserves remain, and can be exploited. It is not on an increase in crop land area, however, but on an increase in the productivity of land already under crop that the prospect of feeding the increasing numbers of the human race depends.

Given adequate water supplies and suitable temperatures, agricultural productivity depends upon the fertility of the soil. Soil is a living system, distinguished from the geological formations beneath by the living flux of growth and decay in plant roots, surface debris, and the soil-inhabiting animals, fungi and bacteria. Its inorganic materials are of geological origin, but its structure, and performance as a nutrient medium for plants, is determined by the climate of the region and the vegetation that grows upon it. It is through the impact of vegetation upon soil that man first gained some control of soil productivity. Much of his experience of soil management has been disastrous, largely because he did not consciously assume responsibility for management. He cleared natural vegetation and planted his crops, and it has taken time and bitter experience to teach him that a soil in balance with natural vegetation inevitably changes, and unless well managed will deteriorate, under cultivation. Hence, much of the world's agriculture has been, indeed still is, exploitive, and it is only in recent years that there has developed an appreciation of the fact that the improvement of agricultural productivity depends upon the domestication and improvement of soils as much as upon the domestication and improvement of crops and stock.

This is not to say that there has in the past been no equilibrium between crops and soil. Equilibria have been established in numerous ways. The earliest and still a common, but long term, balance between soils and crops is that achieved under shifting cultivation. Provided the population does not press excessively on the land, productivity is maintained by the alternation of cropping and regeneration under natural vegetation. By clearing and burning, the nutrient store locked up in the vegetation is released. It is exploited in crop production, and is then reassembled over the long regeneration period, later to be again released by cutting and burning. This is a means of restoring the 'wild' soil, and can never lead to the continuing productivity attainable by a domesticated soil, properly nourished by manuring and management.

In more advanced agricultural systems with the land permanently in cultivation, equilibrium is established if the system is closed and the elements of fertility extracted in the crops are ultimately returned to the land. Moreover, some accretion to fertility arises from the weathering of soil minerals. This last factor varies enormously with the nature of the soil and of the parent geological material. At one extreme are the soils of the world's ancient land masses, completely weathered to great depth, in which there is virtually no increment to fertility from soil minerals. In such soils the fertility store is what is carried in the vegetation and in the top soil, and these are characteristically the soils on which, in the absence of fertilizer supplies from without, only shifting cultivation can be practised. At the other extreme are soils on recent volcanic material, with a vast reserve of young minerals from which nutrient elements are released by weathering. Given an agricultural system in which nitrogen supplies can be built up, normally by including legumes in the rotation, such soils are productive indefinitely. Even on the steep and highly erodible slopes of volcanic cones, continuous, or almost continuous, cropping may be practised. It is with these geological resources that permanent agriculture, carrying a dense population dependent on rice as its staple food, has been established in the volcanic areas of Indonesia, with rainfall that would in other circumstances result in land suited only to tropical forest or plantation crops. Indeed, Indonesia, with soils varying from the very ancient, weathered and leached, to the recent volcanic, with rich reserves of unweathered minerals, provides an excellent illustration of the interaction between rainfall and soil type in determining the productivity of agriculture, and the nature of the farming systems that can be successfully practised.

Between the extremes of ancient poverty-stricken soils suited only to shifting cultivation, and young volcanic soils supporting indefinitely a highly productive agriculture, are a great range of soils that have been exploited and run down to a level at which the casual return of refuse and manure to the land, and the weathering of soil minerals, balance the losses from cropping, leaching and erosion. These are to be found commonly in areas where the balance between water supply and water use is reasonably satisfactory. Under conditions as different as those in England in the Middle Ages, and peninsular India today, these soils remain fairly stable at a yield level of from 500 to 1000 kg of grain per hectare. The worst of them, light sandy soils such as the East Anglian Breck, and the birs of the Malwa plateau in India, degenerated until they went out of cultivation altogether. The best, such as the great alluvia of northern India and West Pakistan, and of the Rhine delta in Europe and the Wash coast in England, have long supported a productive agriculture and a large agricultural population.

Even within this middle belt of stable agricultural land, there have been steady losses throughout agricultural history. Of these losses the most important cause is accelerated erosion. Erosion is a natural and continuous process. Muddy water in the Cam in England is as sure an index of erosion as a gully on the bank of the Jumna in India. Look at any hedge running across the face of a hill in English arable country, and note a difference in level of two feet or more between the top and bottom sides. Erosion goes on in England, but at a rate that is not in excess of the rate of weathering giving rise to new soil to replace the old.

Where soil is bare through long months of a dry season, and is then exposed to violent rainstorms, the rate of soil loss is greatly in excess of the rate of regeneration, and land is lost from agriculture. Losses are greatest where the land is steep, and the most vulnerable land is soon out of cultivation. Unfortunately this does not mean that it is left to natural regeneration, and the re-establishment of a protective cover. Stock keepers regard land that is not in cultivation as grazing and browsing areas, and so the land that has been stripped of its natural vegetation, and much of its soil, remains bare and exposed under the grazing of cattle, sheep and goats. No less important than the loss of soil from the high ground is its deposition on the plains. Silt-laden floods have been a major problem on the irrigation systems of northern India. In 300 years 2 m of stones, gravel, and silt have been washed from the surrounding hills into a valley in Montserrat in the West Indies.

Where rivers are long enough, and have a gentle enough fall, the deposit of river silt may be of value. In western Greece, a very substantial area of valuable alluvial land has been gained during the Christian era by the silting up of a lagoon. The Nile delta has been maintained in fertility over several millennia by the deposit of the finer products of erosion of the Ethiopian highlands. Indeed, irrigated agriculture has been successfully established primarily where such conditions exist, and a deep level alluvium with a good plant nutrient status has been laid down by a slow flowing river. Where irrigation has been established on such a river alluvium, losses of land are commonly the result of the converse of the processes that go on under rainfall conditions. The distribution over the land of irrigation water in excess of crop requirement leads to percolation to the water table, and the water table begins to rise. Rises of as much as 60 m have been recorded over a few decades in India and Pakistan. When the water table reaches levels 1 or 2 m below the surface, drainage problems arise, and evaporation leads to the deposit of salts in the surface layers, and as the salt concentration builds up, crop production goes down and in time the saline lands go out of cultivation.

The study of land deterioration is a recent one, and those who first enquired into it were so impressed with the damage that has resulted from erosion and salination that there arose a belief that land once lost was lost forever, and the basic resources available to mankind were being permanently depleted. In recent years, numerous cases of successful regeneration have been described, and it is apparent that many types of soil can be reclaimed, both from erosion and from salination. In this country the restoration to agriculture of land ruined by opencast mining for coal and for ironstone is an easily observed example. In irrigated areas in many parts of the world, the reclamation of salted land can now be undertaken successfully by drainage and by soil treatments followed by washing out the salts with irrigation water. Erosion can be combated by gully stopping and by the establishment and consistent maintenance of a good plant cover. Badly damaged land does not immediately become productive, but a regenerative cycle can be established, and the productive potential can be steadily built up.

This is the potential, and these are the problems of soils at what may be called a natural level of productivity. There remain for consideration the improvement of soils under domestication, and the establishment of a high level of productivity under skilled management, comparable with that achieved by the domestication and improvement of crops and livestock.

THE IMPROVEMENT OF PRODUCTIVITY

A small, closed farming community turns over the available nutrients with little loss or little gain, but even in a small human community there is always a tendency to concentrate fertility near the homestead. Refuse, hearth ash, and excrement both human and animal, are thrown out near the home, and there arises an area of high fertility that serves as an object lesson in manuring and a demonstration of the rewards that manuring can give. For most of human history, manuring has in fact been a process of fertility transfer. The distant lands, whether they were at the far end of the same farm, or in a far country exporting food in return for industrial goods, were robbed of fertility to raise the productivity of lands nearest the human settlements. So the 'jungle' lands of the Indian village have nourished the 'adhan' lands of the village perimeter, the grain lands of the Baltic fed the farms on the outskirts of the Netherlands towns, and the corn lands of America and the oilseed producing lands of the tropics, the farmlands of England.

Fertility transfer was most successfully practised in western Europe and the United Kingdom. Here, fertility improvement was also practised, by such techniques as liming and marling, and by the invention and development of land drainage. Then in the eighteenth century came the series of innovations in husbandry commonly known as the agricultural revolution of the Norfolk improvers. Cropping systems were altered, and husbandry practices were changed to achieve a standard of weed control higher than ever before, and the feeding of livestock improved enormously. These and other innovations contributed to the great advance in productivity, but were not the key to it. The real change in English farming practice came from the deliberate conservation of all the elements of fertility, and their systematic distribution over the land from which they came. England's farms have gained fertility from overseas right up to the present day, but casual fertility transfer within the farm was replaced by deliberate allocation of manure over the farm as a whole.

The conservation and proper distribution of fertility with the associated intensification of livestock husbandry led to a great improvement in productivity on the light soils of eastern England. On the light lands cultivation is easy and drainage is no problem. Their weakness is their low fertility status, and the careful husbanding of all there was led to great improvement. The heavy clays were not so responsive, and improvement came more from drainage, and from grassland husbandry, particularly in meeting the rising demand for milk in the new industrial towns.

Fertility conservation alone would have been a short lived advance. Farming communities were no longer closed, and there arose a large and increasing drain of fertility to the towns. In the eighteenth century, most town refuse, and indeed excrement, ultimately came back to the land, but as the towns grew, and more especially as they developed modern sanitation systems, the elements of fertility exported from the farms as food ran to waste through disposal systems that ultimately ended in the sea. Nevertheless, it was on the lands that had gained so much from conservation that the next great increase in productivity was mounted.

Fertilizers date from Liebig's experiments and their application to farming practice through the work of Lawes and Gilbert. Through the fertilizer industry, urban communities give back to the land the elements of fertility taken off in crops and stock. Moreover, for the first time it became possible not merely to maintain, but consciously to improve the level of fertility of the land. Increasing knowledge of the composition of soils, and increasing versatility in industrial chemistry, have made it possible to create a new fertility balance in a way that was never possible before. And the rewards in terms of improved productivity have been very large indeed. Yields of cereals in England increased by 30 per cent between 1770 and 1880. They remained stationary for sixty years and then, when the stimulus of wartime and post-war needs led to the full exploitation of new knowledge and new resources in fertilizers and machine power, they increased by 50 per cent in two decades. And they are still increasing.

The achievement of high productivity in England is representative of what has been done in western Europe, North America, and other areas where the western European pattern of agriculture has been established. It has led in the last decade to the accumulation of farm surpluses that have been an embarrassment to the producing countries, and the salvation of millions in countries where no such agricultural revolution has occurred. Most of the rest of the world is practising agriculture at or near the 'natural' fertility level of its soils. While there are limited prospects of increasing the area of land under cultivation, the chances of feeding adequately our increasing numbers depend on the prospects of bringing off productivity revolutions of the kind through which western Europe and America have passed.

The technology of fertility improvement will be very different in different places, but that the potential for improvement is there, there can be no doubt. The limited areas of high fertility in the vicinity of Indian villages, the records of great improvement in research projects in India and Africa, and the advance in productivity achieved in such rural development projects as Shell's Borgo a Mozzano enterprise, are clear enough indications of what can be done. Stagnation is due more to lack of will and lack of communication than to lack of knowledge. Yields in England have increased fourfold in five centuries, and are still increasing at a rate never before equalled. With the knowledge we now have of the technology of increasing productivity, it would not be unreasonable to set as a target a rate of increase in yields double the rate of increase in population over the next fifty years. That is to say, we have the technology to get the rest of the world into the position of food surplus that the West has enjoyed in recent years. We need also the political skills to put the technology into practice, and the foresight and social conscience to stabilize our numbers so that we can maintain that position when it has been established.

CONCLUSION

by J. B. Hutchinson

The lectures on which this volume is based were written and delivered during what may be regarded as the 'food supply decade'. In 1957 the *per capita* production of food in the world's great development areas was recognized as inadequate for the needs of the people. In 1967 *per capita* production was no higher (see Table 9). By contrast, the western world entered the decade with large stocks of food, and accumulated surpluses in North America to an almost insupportable level by 1961. From then on, stocks were run down by massive shipments in aid each year to meet deficiencies in India and Pakistan, and by sales to both the USSR and China in years of serious deficits in those countries (see Table 11). In 1969, thanks to good harvests in countries hitherto in deficit, the balance between food supplies and demand for food looks better than for many years. Stocks in North America are no longer burdensome, and production in the developing countries has improved. Indeed, there are suggestions that the Indian rice crop is so large as to be embarrassing.

Two conclusions may be drawn from this remarkable change in the world situation. The first is that the intensive food production effort, initiated by FAO with the Freedom from Hunger Campaign, has borne fruit. The second is that the hazards of agricultural production are such that large reserve stocks are necessary if human communities are to be secure against famine consequent on climatic adversity. The 'surpluses' that the United States Government found almost unmanageable were in fact no more than enough to meet the world's major deficits within the decade, and leave a workable carryover to the next period. Indeed, it is misleading to regard the stocks that were built up as surpluses.

The need to carry stocks of food as the only possible cover for climatic risk is as old as Joseph and Pharaoh. With improved communications it is now possible to organize the use of food stocks on a global basis, and there is the additional prospect of using the bumper crops of one climatic regime to meet the deficits of another. Nevertheless, the maintenance of adequate stocks is still necessary, and it is unfortunately inevitable that the finance and physical resources to purchase and store surpluses over current market requirements can only be provided by the advanced countries. Thus the security of the world from famine over the past decade has depended on storage made possible by the wealth of the United States. Moreover, the poverty of India results in a bumper rice crop being an embarrassment because it exceeds current demand, and there are not the resources, physical or financial, to provide for storage for future use. There is a need for explicit recognition and study of the problems involved in the provision of stocks against climatic uncertainty. This is a matter for international action, since it is unreasonable to expect that the risks will be covered by a few wealthy countries concerned primarily with the welfare of their own agricultural industries.

The fortuitous—but fortunate—achievement of a rough balance between food supplies and the demand for food makes 1969 a particularly favourable year in which to reassess the population and food supply problem. As King has pointed out, a balance between supply and demand means no more than that there is as much food in the market as can be purchased with the money available. It does not mean that there is enough food to meet all human needs. Thus the real problem, which is poverty, is no longer obscured by the secondary problem, which was inadequate production. Poverty is the cause of hunger and malnutrition as surely in Calcutta and Cairo today as it was in Glasgow and Jarrow at the time of Lord Boyd-Orr's survey in 1936.

King has also drawn attention to the difficulty of ameliorating poverty in circumstances of rapid population growth. Only by improving the equipment of the working population is a real and progressive increase in wealth possible, and while there is a high birth-rate and a high survival rate, the first charge on savings must be for the equipment of the larger new generation.

The great achievement of world agriculture in meeting the effective demand for food will end in frustration unless it is matched by a rate of saving that will make possible a real increase in wealth. Agricultural depression has in the past followed an increase in food production beyond the capacity of the community to buy it. Whether it be by the exploitation of vast virgin lands or by the increase in productivity of existing agricultural areas, rapid increase in food supplies leads to unmanageable surpluses unless the need for food can be translated into effective demand.

Parkes has shown how medical technology has brought down the death-rate in developing as well as in advanced countries, and how in the absence of equal success in what may be termed medical sociology, this has resulted in rapidly growing populations with a heavy weighting in the younger groups. This population structure is the most difficult in which to promote a level of savings that will make possible a real increase in *per capita* wealth. From the essays of Banks and Carpenter it is apparent that the needs of these young populations are particularly high in respect of the most expensive (in terms of agricultural inputs) types of food if population control by biological catastrophe is to be avoided.

Population growth at anything like the current rate cannot be supported for many generations. This is clear. But despite the constraints and rigidities of the current agricultural system, some of which are set out by Allan, there are opportunities now within our reach to increase the world's food supply very substantially. There can be no disagreement with the view that our first obligation is to provide the food and other biological resources for all those already born, or whose arrival we can foresee. In the longer term, however, it should be accepted that agricultural production cannot be multiplied indefinitely. It is no more than common prudence to plan for the stabilization of human populations before the point is reached that food production can no longer keep pace with human multiplication, and readjustment by catastrophe becomes inevitable.

FURTHER READING

ALLAN, W. (1965). *The African Husbandman*. Edinburgh and London: Oliver and Boyd.

BHATIA, B. M. (1968). *Famines in India, 1850–1943*. 2nd ed. New York: Asia Publishing House.

BURGESS, ANNE and DEAN, R. F. A. (1962). *Malnutrition and Food Habits*. London: Tavistock Publications.

CIBA FOUNDATION (1967). *Health of Mankind*. J. and A. Churchill.

CLARK, C. (1967). *Population Growth and Land Use*. London: Macmillan.

CLARK, C. and HASWELL, M. R. (1967). *The Economics of Subsistence Agriculture*. 3rd ed. London: Macmillan.

COONTZ, S. H. (1957). *Population Theories and their Economic Interpretation*. London: Routledge & Kegan Paul.

DAVIDSON, S. and PASSMORE, R. (1966). *Human Nutrition and Dietetics*. 3rd ed. Edinburgh: E. and S. Livingstone.

DOBB, MAURICE, H. (1948). *Soviet Economic Development*. New York: International Publishers.

FARMER, B. H. (1957). *Pioneer Peasant Colonization in Ceylon*. London: Roy. Inst. Intnl. Affairs.

FARMER, B. H. (1963). [published 1966] The Pioneer Peasant in India. *Ceylon Geographer* **17**, 49. Translated as 'Le Paysan Pionnier en Inde'. *Annales Econ. Soc. Civilisations (1967)* **22**, 1227.

FAO (annually). *State of Food and Agriculture*. Rome.

GOUROU, P. trans. LABODE, E. D. (1953, 3rd ed. 1961). *The Tropical World*. London: Longmans.

VON HAGEN, VICTOR W. (1962). *The Ancient Sun Kingdoms of the Americas*. London: Thames and Hudson.

HAUSER, P. M. (ed.) (1963). *The Population Dilemma*. Englewood Cliffs, New Jersey: Prentice-Hall.

HUTCHINSON, J. B. (ed.) (1965). *Essays on Crop Plant Evolution*. Cambridge University Press.

HUTCHINSON, J. B. (1966). Land and Human Populations. *The Advancement of Science* **23**, 1.

KEYS, A. *et al.* (1950). *The Biology of Human Starvation*. Vol. I and II. University of Minnesota Press.

LEACH, E. R. (1961). *Pul Eliya, a Village in Ceylon*. Cambridge University Press.

MEADE, J. E. (1967). Population Explosion, the Standard of Living and Social Conflict. *Economic Journal*, June.

MINISTRY OF AGRICULTURE, FISHERIES AND FOOD (1961). *Manual of Nutrition*. 6th ed. London: HMSO.

MOURANT, A. E. and ZEUNER, F. E. (eds.) (1963). Man and Cattle. Proceedings of a Symposium on Domestication. *Occasional Paper No. 18, Roy. Anthrop. Inst. of G.B. and Ireland*, London.

NICHOLLS, L., SINCLAIR, H. M. and JELLIFFE, D. B. (1961). *Tropical Nutrition and Dietetics*. 4th ed. Baillière, Tindall & Cox.

OHLIN, G. (1967). *Population Control and Economic Development*. Development Centre of the Organisation for Economic Co-operation and Development, Paris.

PARKES, A. S. (1966). *Sex, Science and Society*. Newcastle upon Tyne: Oriel Press.

RAYNS, F. (1961). *A Revolution in Arable Farming*. 3rd Lord Hastings Memorial Lecture. Norfolk Agric. Sta. Norwich: Jarrold & Sons.

SAND RENE. (1952). *The Advance to Social Medicine*. London: Staples Press.

SUKHATME, P. V. (1965). *Feeding India's Growing Millions*. London: Asia Publishing House.

TITMUS, R. and ABEL-SMITH, B. (1961). *Social Policies and Population Growth in Mauritius*. London: Methuen.

UNITED NATIONS (1958). *Future Growth of World Population*.

WIDDOWSON, E. M. and MCCANCE, R. A. (1954). Studies on the Nutritive Value of Bread and on the Effect of Variations in the Extraction Rate of Flour on the Growths of Undernourished Children. *Medical Research Council Special Report Series No. 287*. H.M.S.O., London.

WINSLOW, C. (1952). *Man and Epidemics*. Princeton University Press.

WORLD HEALTH ORGANISATION. Technical Report Series. No. 303 of 1965, Nos. 326 and 332 of 1966 and No. 360 of 1967. Geneva.

WRIGHT, N. C. (1961). *Hunger, can it be averted?* Brit. Ass., London.

YANG, W. Y. (1962). Farm Development in Japan. *Agricultural Development Paper No. 76*. F.A.O. Rome.

INDEX

abortion, birth control by, 21-2, 23-4

Africa, diet in, 53, 64, 83; food production in, 31, 33, 35, 76, 77; foodstuffs trade of, 34, 86; land tenure and agriculture in, 98-101; population of, 7, 8

agriculture, areas of, 125; percentage of population engaged in, vii, 4, 30, 35, 111, 113-14; resources of, 115-34; see also productivity

alluvial soils, 130, 131

Amaranthus spp., as food plants, 118, 119

amino-acids, 72, 73

Anatolia, land tenure in, 102

animals, domesticated, 118, 121

antelopes, possible domestication of, 121

Arachis, as food plant, 118

Argentina, 30, 85

Asia, diet in, 53, 83; food production in, 21, 22; population of, 7, 8, 25

Australia, birth rate in, 25; food from, 30, 33-4, 85; see also Oceania

Aztecs, human sacrifice by, 18

Baltimore, water table near, 5

bananas, 73, 116, 119

barley, 117; regional production of, 76; trade in, 86

Bates, Marston, 10

Berelson, Dr, 27

bilharzia, 13, 51

birth control, 10, 20-5, 46, 58; opposition to, 25-7

birth rates, 4, 7, 13; in developing countries, 57; in England and Wales, 6, 55, 57; industrialization and, 6, 29, 40; low calorie intake and, 69

Boserup, E., 93

Brassica spp., as food plants, 117

breast-feeding, 53, 54, 56

Britain, agricultural productivity in, 30, 36, 94, 132-3; food imports of, 37; land tenure in, 108-9, 110; see also England and Wales, United Kingdom.

Bulgaria, land tenure in, 112

calcium, in diet, 63-5

Calcutta, population of, 4

California, water table in, 5

calories, in diet, 67-71; in national food supplies, 83, 90-1

Canada, anti-birth-control legislation in, 26; food production in, 30, 36, 85

capital, 4, 41-2, 136; for agricultural productivity 110; soil as, 1

carbohydrates, 70

cassava (manioc, tapioca), 70, 73, 119

catastrophe, population control by, 19, 47-50, 137

cellulose, as possible food, 70

censuses, 82

cereals, *see* grains

Ceylon, import of rice by, 95; production statistics for, 78-9, 80, 82

Chaggaland, Tanzania, land tenure in, 102

Chenopodium spp., as food plants, 117, 118, 119

children, death rates of, 53, 56; protein deficiency among, 52-4, 73-4

China, grain imports by, 34, 135; lack of statistics for, 87, 88; (Taiwan), land reform in, 98, 108

cholera, 51

chromosome mechanism, 12

Clark, C., and Haswell, M. R., 82, 84, 90, 91

coitus interruptus, birth control by, 21, 22

collective farms, 111, 112

communal tenure of land, 96-7, 98-101

conception, control of, 22-7

contraceptives, IUCD, 23-4, 58; legislation against, 26; oral, 24-5

cooperative organization in agriculture, 100, 103, 106, 107-8

INDEX

human sacrifice, population control by, 18, 22

Huxley, Julian, 18

India, 45; diet in, 71, 90–1; famines in, 48, 92; food production in, 36, 87, 89, 135, 136; grain shipments to, 34, 38, 135; land reform in, 106; losses of food in, 59, 81; population of, 8, 25, 45; soils of, 130; statistics of food production in, 82

Indonesia, soils of, 129

industrialization, and fertility, 6, 29, 40

infant mortality, 4, 53

infanticide, population control by, 19, 22

infertility, medical attention to, 20

international aid, 10, 38, 39

International Planned Parenthood Federation, 26

iodine, in diet, 54

Iraq, land reform in, 106, 110

Ireland, 30, 50

iron, in diet, 54

irrigation, 112, 123, 128, 131

Italy, land tenure in, 104, 109

IUCD, 23–4, 58

Japan, birth rate in, 21, 22, 25, 58; food production in, 36, 103,

Johnson, Dr, 47

Kenya, land tenure in, 99, 100, 102

Keynes, J. M., 29

Kumar, D., 93

kwashiorkor, 53–4, 73

land, extension of agriculture to new areas, of, 5, 30, 35, 37, 112; under crops, 125

land reform, 93, 101, 105–8

land tenure, and productivity, 93, 96–114.

Latin America, diet in, 53, 64, 83; food production in, 33, 34, 35, 76, 77; foodstuffs trade of, 34, 86; land reform in, 104, 105; population of, 7, 8, 25, 31

Leguminosae, food plants from, 117, 118; nitrogen from, 129

Linum, fibre and oil-seed from, 118

McCance, R., 62

maize, 73, 118; regional production of, 76; trade in, 86

malaria, 51

malnutrition, 52–5

Malthus, T., 1, 6, 28

Manautou, J. M., 22–3

marasmus, 53

margarine, 66

marriage, age at, 20

Marx, Karl, 93

massacre, population control by, 18, 22

Mauritius, population of, 13, 14

meat, regional production of, 76, 87; trade in, 86

menopause, age at, 20

Mexico, land reform in, 107; origin of agriculture in, 116; population of, 16, 42

milk, cow's, 64, 73; regional production of, 76, 87

millets, 117

minerals, depletion of supplies of, 41; in diet, 63–5

natural selection, under-nutrition and, 55

Near East, diet in, 83; food production in, 34, 35, 76, 77; foodstuffs trade of, 34, 86; land tenure in, 101, 102, 104; population of, 8

New York, population of, 4

New Zealand, birth rate in, 25; food from, 30; *see also* Oceania

North America, diet in, 83; food production in, 34, 35, 36, 37, 76, 77, 88; foodstuffs trade of, 33, 86; population of, 8; *see also* Canada, United States

oats, 117

Oceania, diet in, 83; food production in, 76, 77, 88; foodstuffs trade of, 86; population of, 7, 8

oestrogen, inhibition of pregnancy by, 23

oil-seed crops, 70, 115, 117, 118

overcrowding, effects of, 17–18, 40

overeating, diseases due to, 55

Pakistan, 16, 135

142

INDEX